D0275113

DANGEROUS DAYS
ON THE
VICTORIAN
RAILWAYS

By the same author

Dangerous Days in the Roman Empire

DANGEROUS DAYS ON THE VICTORIAN RAILWAYS

*A history of the terrors and the torments,
the dirt, diseases and deaths
suffered by our ancestors*

Terry Deary

Weidenfeld & Nicolson

LONDON

First published in Great Britain in 2014
by Weidenfeld & Nicolson

1 3 5 7 9 10 8 6 4 2

A CIP catalogue record for this book
is available from the British Library.

HB ISBN   978 0 297 87058 6

Printed in Great Britain by
The CPI Group (UK) Ltd, Croydon CR0 4YY

Weidenfeld & Nicolson

The Orion Publishing Group Ltd
Orion House
5 Upper Saint Martin's Lane
London, WC2H 9EA
An Hachette UK Company
www.orionbooks.co.uk

The Orion Publishing Group's policy is to use papers
that are natural, renewable and recyclable products and made
from wood grown in sustainable forests. The logging and
manufacturing processes are expected to conform to the
environmental regulations of the country of origin.

To Jenny Deary
for keeping me on the right track

CONTENTS

INTRODUCTION

'I see that man has bought a British Railways pie.
Must be a stranger around here.'
Character in British sit-com, Oh, Doctor Beeching! *(1997)*

'Sweeping changes will be needed. Effort and
sacrifices will be required from all.'
Ministry of Transport report (1963) which led to the Beeching report

Sweeping changes. They have happened in every era of history. But some are more sweeping than others. Changes so dramatic they have their own memorable dates which must be forcibly etched into the memories of suffering school kids. You know the sort of thing ...

AD 410   The Barbarians invade Rome and the Roman Empire crumbles. (Not really that simple but good enough for school textbooks.)

1066   William the Conqueror and his Normans invade England and have a power base for Crusades that will divide the world to this day.

1349   The Black Death sweeps away rats and humans
        alike.* Surviving peasants are a rare commodity
        and people-power is on the rise.

1485   Richard III is defeated at Bosworth with the last
        great charge of knights on a battlefield – guns will
        defeat lances. And the murderous Tudor family
        will rule and bring in religious reformation.

1825   The Stockton and Darlington Railway becomes the
        first steam railway in the world to carry passengers.
        Stagecoach companies will never be the same again.
        Seaside towns will thrive and human beings will
        find inventive new ways to die.

What drives the changes? In the Roman Empire it was a thirst
for 'Power'. The Normans were seeking 'Glory'. The Peasants'
Revolt was about 'Justice' and the Wars of the Roses back to
the 'Power' thing again. The railway revolution? 'Greed.'

The spidery sprawl of lines on a map were mapped by men
in pursuit of money. Those lines may as well have been drawn
in blood because the cost in human mortality was considerable. And the cost in human *morality* was enormous too. In
the pursuit of the great god gold the railway builders didn't
worry about cheating and lying, using and abusing, betraying
and stealing. Stealing ideas was the railroad to riches.

---

* Yes, the poor rats suffered too. They get the blame for the plague but it
was the fleas that carried the disease. When an infected rat died, the flea
– with no palate for cold blood – hopped onto another passing creature,
like a human being. It's time some revisionist historian campaigned to
restore the reputation of dear *rattus rattus*.

'Capital isn't that important in business. Experience isn't that important. You can get both of these things. What is important is ideas.'

Harvey Samuel Firestone (1868–1938), American tyre manufacturer

There were winners and losers … and winners who ended up losers. There were those who lost bank balances and homes and those who lost their lives.

What sort of miseries did Victoria's railway people suffer? What dangerous days did they have to withstand so we can now get from London to Edinburgh in three hours and forty minutes?

I'm glad you asked …

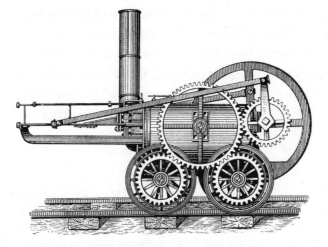

Richard Trevithick's engine

STEAM AND STRUGGLE

> 'The marvel of all history is the patience with which men and women submit to burdens unnecessarily laid upon them by their governments.'
>
> *William Edgar Borah (1865–1940), American statesman*

~ HIT AND MYTH ~

King Alfred burned some cakes ... a myth.

James Watt invented the steam engine – a myth. He 'improved' the steam engine – true.*

Watt was inspired by a tea kettle – myth. Yet it's an enduring myth that still appears in school textbooks:

> 'In the mid-1700s, 12-year-old James sat in the kitchen with his aunt, staring at a tea kettle. As he watched the kettle, James learned about the power of steam.'
>
> *US schools' science book, 2013*

---

* In 1690 Denis Papin built the first steam engine with piston and cylinder. Watt's refinements, such as adding a separate condenser, justifies his reputation. He just didn't 'invent' the steam engine.

It's nonsense. Who dares to argue with an American school textbook? James Watt himself, who said …

> 'My attention was first directed in the year 1759 to the subject of steam-engines by the late Dr Robinson … he at that time threw out the idea of applying the power of the steam-engine to the moving of wheel-carriages, but the idea was not matured.'
>
> *James Watt (1736–1819), Scottish inventor and mechanical engineer*

Watt goes on to explain that he carried out experiments on the force of steam 'about the year 1761' when he'd have been 25 years old. Not a 12-year-old boy-wonder.

Fact file – Steam engines

'Atmospheric Engine': A boiler sends steam into a cylinder with a piston that is pushed up by the steam. Cold water is injected into the cylinder, the steam condenses and creates a vacuum which sucks the piston down. Repeatedly. Wasteful, though, heating that cylinder.

'Watt's Engine': the condensing part takes place in a separate vessel outside the cylinder. This uses a third of the fuel. But that condenser is bulky. Not suitable for mounting on wheels.

Watt took out a cunning patent on his steam engine. Instead of describing it in detail he left it vague …

> 'A new method of lessening the consumption of steam and fuel in fire engines.'

So any other inventor who came up with a 'new method' to improve low-pressure engines was stuffed. It had taken Watt 11 years to develop his idea into a working machine so maybe he deserved to capitalize on his success.

Even Watt didn't solve the problem of 'applying the power of the steam-engine to the moving of wheel-carriages'.* He didn't need to invent the locomotive to pay his pension. He died a wealthy man.

The man who *did* 'apply the power' died in poverty. You could say he died *from* poverty. His name was Richard Trevithick and his tale is a sad one.

> 'Unrewarded genius is almost a proverb; the world is full of educated derelicts.'
>
> *Calvin Coolidge (1872–1933), US president*

While Watt was coupled to the idea of a low-pressure steam engine (a few pounds pressure to the square inch) along came Cornishman Richard Trevithick who was working on a high-pressure engine (around 50 pounds pressure). It would be less bulky and engineers could put the engines on wheels to get a practical steam-driven carriage.

Someone tried to have the British Parliament pass an act *banning* high pressure on the grounds that the public would be in danger from high-pressure engines exploding.

Who was the man that tried to stop the Industrial Revolution in its tracks? He was an icon of the steam age.

---

* After a successful career in selling his improved steam engine, Watt retired to carry on inventing. One successful invention was a machine for copying sculptures. Not a lot of people know that.

Who? Watt. Why? Good question. Three answers …

1   Obviously young Trevithick was a threat to his profits. What do you do if you are a powerful, wealthy person and face some opposition? If a butterfly annoys you? Get your friends to take a shotgun and blast it. After all …

> 'Power without abuse loses its charm.'
>
> *Paul Valéry (1871–1945), French poet and philosopher*

2   Watt always said high-pressure steam engines were lethal. He may have believed it.*

3   But was there another more personal reason? In 1777 Watt had taken his machine to Cornwall to explain how it saved fuel.† A Cornish engineer stood up and poured scorn on Watt's claims. Watt was seething. He wrote …

> 'I was so confounded with the impudence, ignorance and overbearing manner of the man that I could make no adequate defence. Indeed I could scarcely keep my temper which, however, I did to a fault.'

---

* His opposition was so fierce one of his workers, William Murdoch (1754–1839) had to conduct high-pressure trials in secret. He made a steam model which he set off on the unlit road to the church one night. It raced off and the clanking, screeching, hissing, hot and smoking vehicle was met by the vicar on his way home. The confused cleric was convinced he had met a demon from Hell.

† Important in Cornwall because it didn't have its own supplies of coal … and the boilers didn't thrive on a diet of pasties or scones with clotted cream.

The impudent and overbearing man's name? Richard Trevithick Senior. So when the 'ignorant' Cornishman's son threatened his profits was Watt motivated by revenge? Did he mutter, in 1790s vernacular, 'It's payback time, sunshine'?

The suppression didn't work. Parliament refused to pass the law. In fact high-pressure steam WOULD go on to kill quite a few members of the public – as we shall see. But without high-pressure steam power the world would have been a different place.*

Did you know … horse sense

James Watt's early engines needed a secure seal around the piston to work. He experimented with all sorts of materials to get a tight fit. One material he tried was horse muck. It didn't work … probably wasn't stable enough. Hemp proved to be the answer.

What was Trevithick's story?

---

* This is of course no consolation to the people who died from high-pressure boiler explosions while whimpering, 'We should have listened to Watt.'

TEN THINGS YOU OUGHT TO KNOW ABOUT RICHARD TREVITHICK

1 Bad lad

Genius is not always recognized at an early age …

> 'People like me are aware of their so-called genius at ten, eight, nine … I always wondered, "Why has nobody discovered me?" In school, didn't they see that I'm cleverer than anybody in this school? That the teachers are stupid, too? That all they had was information that I didn't need? I used to say to me auntie, "You throw my fuckin' poetry out, and you'll regret it when I'm famous," and she threw the bastard stuff out. I never forgave her for not treating me like a fuckin' genius or whatever I was, when I was a child.'
>
> *John Lennon (1940–80), English singer/songwriter* *

Richard's dad was a mine 'captain', responsible for the steam engines in a Cornish tin mine. If Richard's teacher (like your teacher) told him to work hard, pass the exams and succeed, then the boy ignored him. His school report said …

> 'Richard is a disobedient, slow, obstinate, spoiled boy, frequently absent and very inattentive.'

If you had an acerbic teacher like that you'd want to be 'frequently absent'. Richard learned about steam engines from observing them. A feature of many Victorian engineers.

---

* Of course this is a fine example of Liverpudlian wit and irony. (I think.)

2   High pressure

The precursor of Watt's engine had been the Newcomen 'atmospheric' engine. Watt's patented condenser saved a lot of coal. Apart from selling engines, Watt charged a royalty to engine owners who used his invention – he asked for one-third of the value of the coal saved. The owners of the engines came to resent this. 'Watt a nuisance,' they probably cried.

Trevithick was one of the men looking for a new system that avoided Watt's 'tax'. By cutting out the condenser you sidestepped Watt's patent and made a smaller machine. A high-pressure steam engine was the answer. Trevithick set to work to make one.

> 'Only those who will risk going too far can possibly find out how far one can go.'*
>
> T. S. Eliot (1888–1965), American/British poet

3   Cambourne 1801

Trevithick's first road-going steam carriage ran near Cambourne, on Christmas Eve 1801. It ran well enough but had the longevity of the Trevithick family Christmas turkey. On 28 December the rutted road outside Cambourne threw the steam car into a ditch where driver Andrew Vivian (Trevithick's cousin) abandoned it. A local engineer took up the story …

---

* Which is rather more profound than Dan Quayle's alleged statement: 'If we don't succeed we run the risk of failure.' Sadly the boring truth is that quote was invented by *MAD* magazine.

'The parties adjourned to the hotel and comforted their hearts with a roast goose and proper drinks when, forgetful of the engine, its water boiled away, the iron became red hot and nothing that was combustible remained.'

Davies Gilbert (1767–1839), Cornish engineer and writer *

4 Coalbrookdale 1802

Road-going machines were not the answer. But a year later, at Coalbrookdale in Shropshire, Trevithick saw an alternative. The ore trucks there were pulled on iron rails (by ropes and a stationary steam engine). Perfect. Trevithick mounted a high-pressure steam engine on wheels.

The machine operated in such a way that it would have had a health and safety officer in a dead faint. And they'd have been right to be horrified. Chance-takers are accident-makers, as they say. There was an accident … and a very hasty cover-up. It was so well covered-up we will never know what went wrong.

---

* And you don't need me to tell you Gilbert was the author of a must on every reader's bookshelf, *On the expediency of assigning Specific Names to all such Functions of Simple Elements as represent definite physical properties; with the suggestion of a new term in mechanics; illustrated by an investigation of the Machine moved by Recoil.* If you don't have a copy, you don't know what you're missing.

Did you know … first train and first car

This famous first Coalbrookdale loco was converted to a stationary rope-puller. How are the mighty fallen. But the machine is remembered today in the shape of a replica that runs in a museum near Coalbrookdale. (The victims of its accident, meanwhile, are forgotten.)

Yet Trevithick's engines were maybe NOT the first steam vehicles in the world. A French engineer, Cugnot, had made a self-propelled steam vehicle back in 1769.

The French invented the motor car? But the second prototype demolished a wall, so the French also invented the car accident.

Was Cugnot a loser or a winner in the revolution? A loser. Because another revolution – the French Revolution – stopped his pension and he fled into impoverished exile in Belgium.

5   Greenwich disaster 1803

'That awful power, the public opinion of a nation, is created by a horde of ignorant, self-complacent simpletons who failed at ditching and shoemaking and fetched up in journalism on their way to the poorhouse.'

Mark Twain (1835–1910), American novelist and humorist

Trevithick went on making high-pressure stationary engines and fitted one in a corn mill at Greenwich, London.

It exploded.

Public opinion turned against him. And public opinion can be manipulated, especially in times of tragedy. James

Watt crowed like a rooster on amphetamines, 'I told you so! I did! High-pressure engines are a killer.'

Trevithick knew it was not the engine but human error that caused the accident ... but no one was listening. He explained ...

> 'It appears the boy that had the care of the engine had gone to catch eels in the basement of the building and left the care of the engine to one of the labourers. This labourer saw the engine working much faster than usual and stopped the engine without turning on the safety valve. A short time after being idle it burst. It killed 3 on the spot and one died later of his wounds.
>
> 'I believe Mr Watt is about to do me every injury in his power. They have done their utmost to report the explosion both in the newspapers and in private letters very differently to what it really is.'
>
> *Richard Trevithick, personal letter*

Watt spread his version of the incident far and wide. Isn't it nice when a rich and powerful man does his own dirty work?

> 'I'll win this race fair and square, even if I have to cheat to do it!'
>
> *Dick Dastardly, cartoon character in* Wacky Races *TV series*

Trevithick responded by fitting more safety devices to the high-pressure engines. His damaged reputation would be harder to repair. Salvation came in an unexpected way ...

6 Pen-y-Darren 1804

If at first you don't succeed, try, try again … as Robert the
Bruce didn't say as he didn't watch a spider spinning its web.*
Trevithick tried again and his next effort came from a bizarre
bet.

> 'All human actions have one or more of these seven
> causes: chance, nature, compulsions, habit, reason,
> passion, desire.'
>
> *Aristotle (384–322 BC), Greek philosopher*

Aristotle doesn't mention 'having a bet' as a human motive …
or maybe he'd argue a game of 'chance' covers that. Certainly
a crazy bet led to the most successful railway journey to date.

Richard 'The Tyrant' Crawshay, a bluff Yorkshireman,
owned Cyfarthfa ironworks in Wales. He was an imperi-
ous 65-year-old in 1804. His younger friend and rival was
42-year-old Samuel Homfray who ran Pen-y-Darren works.
We can imagine the bet arose after a few bottles of port had
been imbibed. 'Eeh up, lad, I can build t'steam tram wagon
better than thee.'†

Samuel Homfray accepted the bet (without the Leeds
accent because he was from Worcester). He turned to Trevithick to build a steam locomotive that could haul his trucks
as well as his horses did.

---

* Yes, another myth that is retold in school books to this day as a 'fact'.
There are several caves in Scotland and Ireland that claim to be the
hideout of Scottish nationalist Robert; several places where he allegedly
watched a spider struggle and succeed and inspire him. Luckily today's
children can dump the school textbooks and research the truth about the
wandering spider … on the world-wide web. (I'll get my coat.)
† I extemporize here as I wasn't there at the time.

Trevithick accepted the challenge. 'Tyrant' Crawshay bet young Sam 500 guineas (£525) that Trevithick's steam locomotive could NOT haul 10 tons of iron over the nine miles of the Pen-y-Darren tramway. Crawshay was a canal investor and there are no prizes for guessing how he earned the name 'The Tyrant'. He had no inkling of the damage the railways would eventually do to the trade on his canals.*

Of course Trevithick's Pen-y-Darren locomotive was to be a high-pressure steam machine with the exhaust steam puffing up the chimney. This drew air through the fire, making it burn hotter to create more steam to replace that just used. Genius.† But would it work and who would win the bet between these business magnates?

> 'The gambling known as business looks with austere disfavour upon the business known as gambling.'
>
> *From* The Devil's Dictionary *by Ambrose Bierce (1842–1914), American author and satirist*

On 21 February 1804 the locomotive set off to huge interest from the locals. They climbed aboard. All the fun of the fair. It hauled 25 tons plus 70 passengers, who hitched a ride.‡ Trevithick believed it could haul loads of 40 tons. As well as

---

* Don't feel too sorry for The Tyrant. He died with £1.5 million in the bank. The Tyrannized couldn't even count that far let alone envisage such riches beyond the dreams of avarice.

† Fatally, Trevithick did not patent his exhaust-steam invention, which became known as the 'blast pipe'. You can't imagine men like Watt or Crawshay making that expensive error. Every steam loco uses Trevithick's 'blast pipe' idea. It lost Trevithick a fortune and could have earned him an early grave.

‡ This was 1804. You'll remember that 1825 is celebrated as the first passenger rail journey from Darlington to Stockton. The 70 'passengers' on Trevithick's train didn't pay for tickets so maybe that's why they don't count in the record books?

proving the blast pipe was efficient, this trip also proved that a smooth wheel could run on smooth rails. Sadly the weight of the loco repeatedly broke those rails so it was never put to regular use.

What happened to the victorious loco? Again it was converted into a stationary engine. Oh the ignominy.

Writing history is a low-paid occupation because it is just relating the past. Predicting the future is priceless. And some nameless journalist on the *Cambrian* newspaper had a brilliant flash of insight when he reported the Pen-y-Darren run …

> 'It is not doubted but that the number of horses in the kingdom will be very considerably reduced, and the machine will be made use of in a thousand instances never yet thought of for an engine.'
>
> *The* Cambrian, *24 February 1804*

How perceptive was that?

And the bet? The stake-holder (referee) did enough hair-splitting to back-comb the bet into a beehive hair-do.

> 'Some of the rails were removed to let the loco pass through a low tunnel … the train didn't return the trucks at the same time as a horse, and the road is not in the same place as when the bet was made.
>
> *Mr Hill, Stake-holder (1804)*

Crawshay didn't get rich by conceding £525 bets without a fight.*

---

* You have to wonder if Crawshay didn't slip the stake-holder a fiver to void the bet? Cynical, moi?

Trevithick's breakthrough bet winner didn't secure his fortune. Still he was pleased to have swung public opinion his way …

> 'The public until now called me a scheming fellow but now their tone is much altered.'
>
> *Richard Trevithick, diary entry 22 February 1804*

Watt's thoughts are nor recorded.*

7   The Newcastle connection 1805

Trevithick's restored reputation brought in more offers to create locomotives than he could personally build. So, for a coal mine in Tyneside, he simply supplied the designs and instructions.

He did manage a trip to Newcastle to supervise the build and there he almost certainly met an inquisitive young man called George Stephenson. We shall hear more of that young man later …†

The Newcastle loco was a modest success but ran on wooden rails which splintered under the weight – and who can blame them? The mine owners were discouraged and decided it was cheaper to feed horses for power than effect the deforestation of the North to replace rails.

It was that meeting with Stephenson that could have been key to the history of Victoria's railways.

---

* Perhaps, in the words of Dick Dastardly, 'Drat! Double drat! And triple drat!'

† Too enigmatic? All right, 'See Chapter 2'. Better?

> 'Good artists copy, great artists steal.'
>
> *Pablo Picasso (1881–1973), Spanish painter, sculptor* *

If Watt was the good artist of 'improving' then Stephenson was the great artist.

8   Catch Me Who Can 1808

In 1805 Trevithick moved to London and tried his hand at tunnelling under the Thames. Despite many ingenious solutions to the problems he encountered, he failed.

The days of the Luddites were fast approaching when workers would rise up against the steam machines making them redundant. When Trevithick invented a steam-powered crane to lift loads at Thames docks the workers protested. When I say 'protested', I mean they threatened to drown the inventor. He was given a police guard and two more officers to protect his house.

> 'A reactionary is a somnambulist walking backwards.'
>
> *Franklin D. Roosevelt (1882–1945), US president*

Then Trevithick made his costliest mistake. He went into partnership with a chancer called Robert Dickinson. In 1808 this man bankrolled the patents for some of Trevithick's inventions. Dickinson would let Trevithick bear the millstone of bankruptcy in 1811.†

---

* This is the man who also said, 'I do not seek, I find.' That is so profound, so deep, I don't understand it.
† It would take him three years to clear the debts. It must have been a powerful persuader towards his abandoning the country.

'An insincere and evil friend is more to be feared than a wild beast; a wild beast may wound your body, but an evil friend will wound your mind.'*

Buddha (563–483 BC), Indian teacher

In 1808 Trevithick built a demonstration railway in a small circle. It was located near the present-day Euston Square tube station. For the massive price of five shillings you could ride a small circular track behind a loco called *Catch me who can*. At 12 miles per hour it would have left quite a few trailing in its smoke … until its weight smashed a rail and it was derailed. *Then* your dead great-grandmother could have caught it. Tortoise and the hare.

9 Peru 1816

'History repeats itself, and the unexpected always happens; how incapable must Man be of learning from experience.'

George Bernard Shaw (1856–1950), Irish-born British playwright

The unexpected always happens. Look at the twists of fate that took Trevithick to Peru.

➤ The ancient silver mines were flooded and unworkable. Swiss merchant Francisco Uvillé set off to find a steam pump to drain them … and make his fortune. He went to the home of steam power, England.

---

* Buddha omitted, 'And wound your credit rating.' Obviously he wasn't a material guy.

➤ James Watt turned down the golden opportunity to make silver. His low-pressure machines wouldn't work at 14,000 feet above sea level. Anyway, they were too cumbersome to carry up the mazy mule trails to the mines. The end? No. Cue Tale of the Unexpected, Episode 1.

➤ Uvillé was desolate and disappointed after meeting Watt. As he headed home he passed a shop window in London that was displaying a working model of Trevithick's high-pressure engine. He took it back to Peru and it worked. Now all he had to do was track down the inventor.*

➤ As Uvillé set sail for England he chatted to passengers about his mission to find Trevithick. Tale of the Unexpected, Episode 2: One of the passengers was Richard Trevithick's cousin. He directed the Swiss to Cornwall. Within a year the pumping and winding engines were ready to set sail. But the engineers lacked the experience to get them working. So ...

➤ In 1816 Trevithick himself set off for Peru. His adventures would fill a book ... though they would appear stranger than fiction.† His mine schemes flourished then came to nothing. By 1827 he became the first

---

* Google, Wikipedia or Facebook had not been invented then, so it was trickier than it sounds.

† They included being conscripted into Simon Bolivar's rebel army, being robbed of his money and abandoning a fortune in ores that he'd worked so hard to mine. His machines were damaged in the civil war but he recovered his fortune with a diving expedition to recover brass cannon from a sunken warship. He then invested his fortune in a wacky pearl-fishing scheme in Panama ... and lost it all again. Robert Louis Stevenson couldn't have made it up.

European to cross the isthmus of Nicaragua as he made his way home. In the process he almost drowned and survived by eating monkeys while avoiding being eaten by alligators until a passing pig-hunter came to his rescue.

➤ Again, by chance, he met Robert Stephenson as he sought a passage home from Cartagena. He was loaned £50 for the sea trip by Robert.*

10 Decline and Fall

'Today's history is yesterday's news.' *Anon*

By 1827 Richard Trevithick was home and broke. He was offered £8,000 for his mineral rights in South America. He thought he could get a better offer and declined. No better offer materialized. He ended with nothing. Again.

By the time Trevithick set foot in England, George Stephenson had opened the Stockton and Darlington Railway and was the darling of the railway phenomenon. The Industrial Revolution was whirling like a spinning jenny. Trevithick, whose high-pressure engines made so much of the Revolution possible, had been wandering the jungles of South America seeking silver. Fools' gold.

---

* Robert's own journey home was hindered by hurricanes. First his vessel had to stop and help damaged ships. On one the starving crew had resorted to cannibalism. Then a storm carried away most of his luggage and all of his money before he reached New York. As his ship struggled he was denied a place in a lifeboat – instead it went to a third-class passenger. Why? Because that passenger, like the mate in charge, was a Freemason. As soon as he landed, the rueful Robert joined the Freemasons. A funny handshake can save your life.

The real gold was his high-pressure steam engine which, by 1825, was commonplace. The world had moved on. He was yesterday's news, old hat, unhip, démodé, past his prime and passé as a Polaroid camera in the digital age.*

His Peru adventure had caused him to miss the train, so to speak. He tried to claim royalties on the high-pressure steam engine patents but failed. Among the greatest defaulters were his fellow-countrymen in the Cornish mines.

In a lecture to mark the centenary of Trevithick's death a professor claimed …

> 'In his own county of Cornwall he was looked up to with a veneration which savoured almost of idolatry, but drew the line at votive offerings.'
>
> *Professor Charles Inglis (1933)*

Oh how the professor's audience must have laughed at that witty remark. But sadly, Prof, it wasn't that funny. Money talks louder than sentiment.

> 'When you're out of sight for as long as I was, there's a funny feeling of betrayal that comes over people when they see you again.'
>
> *Esther Williams (1921–2013),*
> *American competitive swimmer and movie actress*

His career was heading for a train crash.

---

* The word 'passé' was originally borrowed from the French to describe a woman past the period of greatest beauty. That's pretty cruel. Trevithick's own descent to being past his period of greatest use must have been cruel.

Old wisdom has it that there are 5 stages in a creative person's career.

1: Richard who?
2: Ah, Richard Trevithick.
3: Get me Richard Trevithick.
4: Get me a young Richard Trevithick.
5: Richard who?

By 1827 Trevithick was hovering between 4 and 5 you'd guess?

New inventions like his recoil mechanism for a gun were modelled but never developed. His concept of a fridge-freezer was genius, and would have made him one of history's heroes, but no one was listening.*

> 'All I ask is the chance to prove that money can't make me happy.'
>
> *Spike Milligan (1918–2002), Anglo-Irish comedian*

Trevithick's weakness was having little business sense and trusting the back-stabbers in the world of engineering.

Trevithick was famed for his phenomenal strength. He could throw sledge-hammers further than anyone, lift full barrels that three men struggled to move, write his name on a high beam while having half a hundredweight strapped to his thumb … you get the idea. His exploits are legendary and they can't all be apocryphal. Yet this strong, fit man was brought down by poverty.

---

* The Georgians understood the value of freezing stuff, you understand. But their solution was to drag large quantities of ice from the Arctic … a Titanic task.

In London the rising star, George Stephenson, petitioned Parliament to give Trevithick a pension in recognition of his contributions to the wealth of the industrial nation. Parliament refused.

In 1828 he was invited to Holland to assist with a scheme to drain the submerged land by the Zuyder Zee. He was so poor he had to borrow 40 shillings for the trip. On the road to the docks he met a poor man who said, 'Help a poor man, my pig has died.' Trevithick gave him five of the precious shillings.

Generous? Or improvident? His work was as brilliant as ever but the directors of the Dutch project fell out and it didn't happen in Trevithick's lifetime. The government gave grants to inventors but the Cornishman was refused one.

Disappointment would have driven lesser mortals from Zuyder to cider. Still Trevithick pressed bravely ahead.

- A steam-powered room heater was a success in 1830 ... but not a great money-spinner.

- A 1,000-foot, cast-iron monumental tower was designed but never built.

- The jet-propelled ship (water-jet) was never built either. It was to be the last patent he applied for.

In April 1833 he went to Dartford to assist a young engineer, John Hall, with an engine design. He would not live to see it completed.

‒ POOR RICHARD ‒

> 'A light purse is a heavy curse.'
>
> Poor Richard's Almanack *(1745)*

Trevithick was taken ill with pneumonia and had to retire to bed at the Bull Hotel, Dartford, where he was lodging at the time. Following a week's confinement in bed he died on the morning of 22 April 1833. He was penniless, and no relatives or friends had attended his bedside during his illness. A Victorian called pneumonia 'the captain of the men of death' – in other words, a top killer.

How could he be brought so low so quickly?

DANGEROUS DAYS DEATH I

PNEUMONIA

Victim: Richard Trevithick

Your lungs are an ideal place for bacteria to grow, but normally they stand no chance against your immune system, which kills them quickly. However if you live in poverty, become weak or don't eat your greens then your immune system is not up to scratch and the pesky blighters can have a field day once you have breathed them into your lungs, which fill up with a mixture of fluid and pus. It is known commonly as pneumonia.

You develop a very high temperature and cough up mugfuls of sticky, green, blood-stained flob (sputum). As the infection spreads the lining of the lungs is affected, breathing becomes harder and you get a very sharp pain every time you breathe in (pleurisy). Finally, overcome by the rampant infection, lungs drowning in pus, struggling for every breath, you gasp your last.

Dr Peter Fox MB, ChB, FRCGP, DrCOG *

As poverty is a bacteria's best friend, you could argue Trevithick died of poverty. His colleagues at Hall's works made a collection for his funeral expenses and acted as bearers. They also paid a night watchman to guard his grave at night to deter grave robbers, as body-snatching was common at that time.

'All geniuses die young.' †

Groucho Marx (1890–1977), American comedian

Trevithick was buried in an unmarked grave in St Edmunds Burial Ground, East Hill, Dartford. The burial ground closed in 1857, with the gravestones being removed in the 1960s. A plaque marks the approximate spot believed to be the site of the grave.

There is a plaque at the Royal Victoria and Bull Hotel, marking Trevithick's last days in Dartford and the place of

---

* Between you and me I thought Dr Peter made that last one up, but I checked and it means 'Diploma of the Royal College of Obstetrics and Gynaecology'. Now we know.

† Richard Trevithick was 62 years old. Will Shakespeare was just 52. So, if you live to collect your pension you're no genius ... and if you collect a telegram from the queen/king on your hundredth birthday you must be several prawns short of a cocktail? Hmmm. Maybe Groucho's theory needs to be treated with caution.

his death in 1833. The Blue Plaque is prominently displayed on the hotel's front.

It's not much of a memorial for the man whose genius shaped Britain and the world.

> 'To every man his little cross. Till he dies.
> And is forgotten.'
>
> *From* Waiting for Godot *by Samuel Beckett (1906–89),*
> *Irish playwright*

BRIEF TIMELINE – THE 1800s

1801   At New Year Britain and Ireland unite and a new flag is created – the Union Jack. Christmas Eve and Richard Trevithick tries out his Puffing Devil steam carriage in Cambourne. Three days later it self-destructs due to driver error. Bah humbug.

1802   A new law says children must not work more than a 12-hour day. In France Napoleon is elected Consul for life. He'll be trouble.

1803   Trevithick demonstrates a steam carriage in London but no one is impressed. When one of his high-pressure engines blows up in a Greenwich mill his competitors make sure the public know how dangerous this man's machines are. Britain goes to war with Napoleon's France. 'United Irishmen' rebel against the union and attack Dublin Castle. Defenders simply close the gates. Rebels go home.

1804   Trevithick's locomotive hauls a coal train on rails for five miles. The first steam-railway trip. The 'Cow-pock Institution' opens in Dublin to develop the smallpox vaccine. Anti-slavery laws passed in the Commons ... while allowing four-year-old Brit boys to climb chimneys and sweep them. Children under seven still working in mills up to 18-hour days.

1805   George Stephenson (a low-pressure steam-engine operator from Tyneside) meets high-pressure steam-engine expert Trevithick. Meanwhile Admiral Nelson is getting himself shot at Trafalgar. Income tax rises to over sixpence in the pound to pay for the Napoleonic War.

1806   A new steam loom in Manchester will transform the cotton industry and ruin the living wage of weavers.

1807   Cotton workers petition for a 'minimum wage'. Now there's a novel idea.

1808   Trevithick's *Catch Me Who Can* locomotive pulls spectators at 12 mph around a circular track in London. The first steam-powered fairground ride?

1809   A young Duke of Wellington is making his name fighting the French in Spain. He's one to watch for the future.

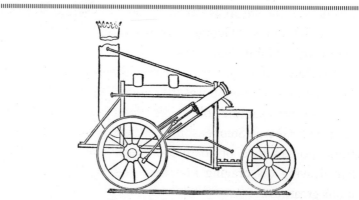

George Stephenson's *Rocket*

ENGINEERS AND EXPLOSIONS

> 'Every positive value has its price in negative terms …
> the genius of Einstein leads to Hiroshima.'
>
> *Pablo Picasso*

> 'Don't be too timid and squeamish about your
> actions. All life is an experiment.'
>
> *Ralph Waldo Emerson (1803–82), American poet*

The 1810s were the age of experiment. Trial and error. Unfortunately the errors could be fatal for some. The geniuses of the steam age created some dangerous days for many. The genius of George Stephenson leads to the death of engine driver John Cree.

The killer machine was George Stephenson's second-most-famous creation. It was the engine, *Locomotion No. 1*.

Before we examine John Cree's fatal last moments let's start with George Stephenson – a slippery character whom train-spotters love or loathe, depending on where they live. Having disparaging knockers doesn't detract from a man's greatness.

> 'When a true genius appears, you can know him by
> this sign: that all the dunces are in a confederacy
> against him.'
>
> *Jonathan Swift (1667–1745), Anglo-Irish satirist*

Stephenson's critics say he was an ignorant northern peasant who never invented anything worthwhile – he just took other people's inventions and made them work better. A mere mechanic. His supporters say he was a brilliant craftsman. He was certainly a hard worker.

> 'God gives talent. Work transforms talent into genius.'
>
> *Anna Pavlova (1881–1931), Russian ballerina*

THINGS THAT GEORGE STEPHENSON DIDN'T INVENT
– NO. 1 – THE LOCOMOTIVE –

In 1836 George Stephenson was called 'The Father of the Locomotive' … and the accolade has stuck for almost 200 years like a gnat to flypaper. In a tribute to Stephenson one Dr Dionysus Lardner* gave him the 'Father of the Locomotive' title.

Yet one of Geordie's biographers put it succinctly:

> 'The fact must be faced that George Stephenson
> himself was largely responsible for initiating the
> legend that he was [the locomotive's] sole parent.'
>
> *L.T.C. Rolt*, George and Robert Stephenson: The Railway Revolution

---

* If a man with a name like Dr Dionysus Lardner says something you are going to believe him, aren't you?

Geordie Stephenson never *claimed* to have invented the locomotive, you understand ... he let other people say it for him. He simply chose not to credit men like Trevithick who *did* do the inventing.

In 1814 George Stephenson saw a loco in action and persuaded the manager of the Killingworth Colliery to let him to build a steam-powered locomotive. This was ten years after Trevithick's first high-pressure engine ran at Pen-y-Darren Colliery.

He built the *Blücher*.

But 'The Father of the Locomotive'? Sorry, Geordie, no.

BRIEF TIMELINE – THE 1810s

1811   As Trevithick struggles with bankruptcy young Timothy Hackworth in the North-East is building his first locomotives. British workers are on the march against the machines. They claim their leader is Ned Ludd (who is as debatably 'real' as Robin Hood). Steam power is replacing manpower and starving the workers, the Luddites claim.

1812   Napoleon retreats from Moscow and London is lit by gas lamps. A first for Britain: Prime Minister Perceval is assassinated. Another first: steamship *Comet* is launched on the Clyde. John Blenkinsop and Matthew Murray of Newcastle run a 'rack' locomotive, *Salamanca*. These locomotives run for another 20 years before the last one finally explodes.

1813   In 1813 William Hedley designs a locomotive that runs on smooth rails, but it just doesn't have enough steam power. THAT is probably the machine George Stephenson sees and declares, 'I could build a better one.'

1814   Napoleon abdicates and is exiled to Elba. Britain and France sign treaty of 'Perpetual peace and friendship'. Yeah. Right.

1815   George 'Geordie' Stephenson invents a miners' safety lamp and makes his name AND the name of the local people.* Meanwhile Napoleon is facing his Waterloo (and loses the Eurovision contest, unlike ABBA). Peace in Britain ... except for London riots over high corn prices.

1816   Trevithick leaves to develop steam pumps in Peru and will be gone more than ten years. The Industrial Revolution will go full steam ahead with his ideas ... but without filling his purse. Greece loses its marbles to Lord Elgin and a new dance shocks *The Times* – it is the waltz.

1817   Violent protests against corn prices – rick-burning and machine-smashing – and the Prince Regent has a stone thrown at him in his carriage.

1818   Edward Pease, a Darlington merchant, proposes a railway line from the Durham coalfields to the port of Stockton. Fierce objections from landowners who fear their cows will be scared and their fox-hunting ruined, horses rendered extinct, birds poisoned and hens stop laying. Londoners riot (again) over poor quality of their beer while Manchester's (united) mill workers strike for more pay.

1819   A peaceful protest meeting in Manchester is attacked by yeomanry and 11 people killed. In a mockery of Waterloo the massacre at

---

* The 'Geordies' not the 'Stephensons'. Don't be flippant. Geordies of Tyneside still bear that name to this day ... as well as several other names applied to them by the folk of neighbouring Wearside.

St Peter's Field will be known as 'Peterloo'.
James Watt dies. No connection.

1820   Stephenson builds Hetton Colliery railway –
the first railway to use no muscle power. Twenty
thousand slaves are sent from Angola to work in
Brazil. Muscle power not dead yet then? George
III dies after 60 years on the throne. Cato Street
Conspirators (the new Guy Fawkes-style plotters)
are beheaded.

THINGS THAT GEORGE STEPHENSON DIDN'T INVENT
– NO. 2 – THE RAILWAYS –

When Geordie wasn't being called the 'Father of the Loco-motive' he was being called the 'Father of the Railways'. But was he?

In British mines there had been trucks running on wooden rails for many years.* Fifty years before Geordie was born there was a horse-drawn railway running from Causey pits in North Durham to the waiting ships on the River Tyne.†

---

* Sometimes called tram-ways, waggon-ways or wagon-ways as well as railways.
† Causey Arch is there to this day. In 1726, it was the longest single-span bridge in the country. Local legend says the architect was sure it would collapse under the weight of coal trucks. To avoid the disgrace he threw himself off the arch to his death when it was complete. Neat tale of tragedy and irony? Sadly it's not true. Architect Wood died in Stockton in 1730 ... four years and 32 miles after he jumped. Long jump. Another myth bites the dust.

Geordie DID expand the rail networks around northern mines and replaced horses with steam-powered winding engines. In the 1820s Stephenson was hired to build an 8-mile (13-km) railway from Hetton Colliery to Sunderland. It opened in 1822 and used locomotives – the first railway in the world using no animal power. It just wasn't the first 'railway' – i.e. vehicles running on rails.

What about the concept of *railways* – 'a network of rail lines'? Did he father that?

Famously, in 1825, Geordie launched the Stockton and Darlington Railway. Undoubtedly the first passenger railway service in the world. But was it his 'idea'? No.

Coal owners wanted to get the black stuff from the hills of Durham down to the coast. Canals worked well, but were painfully slow and expensive to build, especially if there were steep inclines that needed locks. So as early as 1810 the Pease Brothers of Darlington proposed a horse-drawn tramway. It would run from the coalfields in the Durham hills to the North Sea port at Stockton. About 40 miles.

Edward and Joseph Pease were bankers and wool merchants, not mine owners, but a tramway would be a good investment.

The Pease family were Quakers and their social consciences drove their scheme. They didn't just want profits, they wanted cheap coal for all. They had envisaged social benefits.

> 'A business that makes nothing but money is a poor business.'
>
> *Henry Ford (1863–1947), American industrialist*

Luckily for Geordie a financial failure of the Durham banks, and objections from landowners, delayed the plan till 1818.*
And by that time locomotives were showing their prowess.

By 1821 the legalities were sorted and they wanted someone to plan and build the railway. Edward Pease met George Stephenson and the rest is history.† Stephenson agreed to take on the job as Engineer.

At the next meeting of the railway group Pease enthused …

> 'If the railway be established and succeeds, as it is to convey not only goods but passengers, we shall have the whole of Yorkshire and next the whole of the United Kingdom following with railways.'

What a vision. A rail *network*. Yet it wasn't George Stephenson's vision. It was Edward Pease's …

Edward Pease … 'Father of the Railway' anyone?‡

---

* The Duke of Cleveland led the protests because of the damage a railway would do to his fox-hunting. Parliament rejected the plan. The line was redrawn to divert around his lordship's foxholes. The plan was then passed. Feudalism was alive and well in County Durham and Westminster.

† Edward Pease took one look at George Stephenson and said, 'I have some knowledge of craniology and from what I see of your head you are the man to successfully carry this through.' Craniology? The 'science' concerned with the shape and size of the human skull. A bizarre way to assess an employee, but it worked.

‡ Oddly the Institute of Mining Engineers STILL calls Stephenson 'Father of the Railways' on its website. So does Wikipedia and quite a few school books.

STOCKTON AND DARLINGTON TRIUMPH OVER TRIBULATIONS

Loco no go

It was a landmark in the history of the world. A 1066 moment. The opening of the Stockton and Darlington Railway. Not only is it historically significant but people at the time recognized the importance too ... some more enthusiastically than others.

> 'The skies rang with loud hurrahs. The happy faces of some, the vacant stares of others and the alarm on the faces of quite a few gave variety to the picture.'
>
> *Eyewitness account*

The observer didn't mention the sour and hostile faces. Those must have belonged to the local press reporters ...

> 'Who would think of paying to be carried in a coal wagon, along a tedious wagon-way by a roaring steam engine?'
>
> Tyne Mercury *newspaper, November 1824*

The answer was, most of the world.

By 1825 the line from Stockton to Darlington was completed. Geordie Stephenson had done a superb job. There was just one last piece to fit in place. It was a piece that YOU would probably put first.

This may seem hard to believe. But when the line was ready the thing that Stephenson lacked was a *locomotive* to pull that first, historic train. A pub-with-no-beer moment.

Geordie Stephenson had usually had his locomotive designs built by William Losh's company. That company also made the cast-iron rails. When Stephenson decided to use wrought-iron rails instead, Losh was furious. It was a massive blow to the Losh business. He retaliated in the best way he knew. He said, 'No rails? No locomotive.' Oh, Joseph, talk about cutting off your arm to spite your hand.

But George carried on.

> 'Never interrupt your enemy when he is making a mistake.'
>
> *Napoleon Bonaparte (1769– 1821), French military and political leader*

Stephenson's way around the problem was typical of the man. He set up his own locomotive factory with son Robert in Forth Street, Newcastle.

Son runs

Then a second setback. In 1824, a year before the S&DR opened, young Robert went off to a new job in Columbia. There's no evidence of a rift with his father, but it's the most likely explanation for a trip to Columbia at such a key moment in their careers. Cantankerous George and a son who'd inherited his stubborn streak? Fathers pass on all they know to their sons, who exploit it.

> 'I am an expert of electricity. My father occupied the chair of applied electricity at the state prison.'
>
> *W. C. Fields (1880–1946), American comedian*

No Robert? No locomotive … and time was pressing now.

Geordie relied on employee Timothy Hackworth and a Liverpudlian, James Kennedy, at the Forth Street works to provide the engine. Building a new locomotive from scratch would be a near impossible task. The solution was staring them in the back.

In the corner of the works young Robert had left a half-finished experimental engine called *Active*. Kennedy finished it and changed the name to the one every train-spotter knows … *Locomotion No. 1*.

It was delivered to the south Durham line for testing.

No one had a match to light the fire under the boiler. A pub with no beer OR beer glasses.

An assistant was sent off to bring a lantern from the village. But it was a sunny day so an old rail worker took out the magnifying glass he used to light his pipe.

> 'Build a man a fire, and he'll be warm for a day. Set a man on fire, and he'll be warm for the rest of his life.'
> *Terry Pratchett (1948—), English fantasy author*

Locomotion No. 1 was fired up and set off with a carriage for the directors. The Pease family were the first railway passengers in the world. They had earned the right.

A grand day out

The big public launch day was 27 September 1825. Thousands of people crowded around the starting point and lined the route. When the safety valve let out a screaming cloud of steam the crowds panicked. But *Locomotion* was not going to explode.*

---

* Well, not today at any rate.

Around 500 people crowded into specially adapted coal trucks and they set off. They had travelled a few hundred yards when one of the trucks came off the rails. It was lifted back on. Off they went for another few hundred yards and it happened again. The faulty truck was shunted off onto a loop … and a spectator was hurt.

Off they went for a few miles … until *Locomotion No. 1* itself broke down … a fouled valve.

The world's first-ever passenger train was going to be nearly an hour late.*****

Eyewitness W. Fallows later reported …

> 'The whole train moved at a rate of 10–12 miles per hour, with an estimated weight of 86 tons. It was computed that about 700 people were drawn in this train, a number which created the greatest astonishment.'

There were 40,000 people waiting in Stockton for the (late) train which rolled in at 3.45 p.m. The dignitaries headed for the town hall where a banquet went on till midnight. They drank 23 toasts that night … which is binge drinking on a corporate scale. The last was drunk to the health of George Stephenson.

He was the toast of the town.

---

* A late train. Imagine how inconvenient that would be if it happened today? 'It was on the old Eastern Counties railway that the tale was originally told of how a ticket collector was expostulating with a strapping lad of sixteen. He could scarcely be entitled to travel at half-rate. The collector was met by the crushing reply that the lad was under fourteen when the train started.' John Aye, *Railway Humour*, 1931.

Did you know …

The S&DR owned the tracks but did not run trains. That's like Network Rail today but with rather less regulation. You paid your money and could haul steam- or horse-drawn wagons on the S&DR's line.

Because there was no timetable the trains ran whenever they wanted. Fights often broke out over rights of way when rival companies met head on. Heavy coal trains were supposed to have precedence over passenger trains and the latter were expected to back up to the nearest loop. Annoying.

Often horse-drawn met steam-drawn. But there are no reports of a horse being punched.*

Passengers often jumped down and helped the driver in his fist-fight with rival drivers.

The victim: John Cree

'In this business it takes time to be really good – and by that time, you're obsolete.'

Cher (1946—), American singer

---

* A Newcastle United football fan who punched a police horse in the head during a riot in April 2013 said in his defence, 'I love animals – I've got three dogs, a fish pond out the back and I feed foxes across the road.' He added, 'I would like to apologize to the horse.' (You couldn't make it up.) Nice to know he doesn't (apparently) punch his fish – thank cod. Fish suffer enough from being battered. A judge with horse sense jailed him for 12 months.

As a piece of steam technology *Locomotion No. 1* was almost obsolete when it achieved immortality on 27 September 1825.

You may imagine the old locomotive would have been retired, showered in honours, to a perch on a plinth in some museum. But that wasn't the ethos of the Industrial Revolution. *Locomotion No. 1* kept working for many years, with one disastrous result.

The early safety valves, designed to relieve the steam pressure and avoid explosions, operated with a weight. When the pressure was high enough the steam lifted the weight and released the precious power. Simple, but it worked.

Driver John Cree was a star of the Stockton and Darlington Railway. He was one of a team of five who could be hired to drive the locomotives, so he was always in demand. The hours were long and the work hard – muscle-straining, deafening, teeth-rattling, sweaty and stressful. As you'd expect the rewards were generous.

In April 1828 Driver John earned 22 pounds, 5 shillings and 5 pence for his labour. And for his skill. Getting the best out of *Locomotion No. 1* was a tricky task. When it was first built the engine's performance was disappointing. Sixty-five years later the president of the Institution of Mechanical Engineers reported ...

'When first put to work *Locomotion No. 1* would not make steam, and the fire tube had to be replaced by a return tube similar to what is now used in the North Country class of tug-boats.'

Joseph Tomlinson, Presidential Address (1890)

Locomotion No. 1 was delivered in time for the opening of the Stockton and Darlington line and still didn't appear to be up to the job. The old workman who lit her fire with a magnifying glass put it even more graphically ...

> 'Eight wagons was as many as she could trail.'
>
> The Diaries of Edward Pease

This 'tug-boat' of a locomotive was expected to pull 22 packed passenger trucks and ten loaded coal wagons. There were to be 120 metres of train behind. Yet *Locomotion No. 1* could manage only 8 wagons?

Somehow George Stephenson and his brother, James, coaxed the engine into giving enough power to make that crucial first journey. Of course, once the opening day was over, Geordie was too busy to spend his days as a driver.* Years passed and traffic from Stockton to Darlington grew.

Locomotion No. 1 was temperamental. Within a month of the grand opening a cast-iron wheel cracked. And for the driver there was always the problem of keeping up *Locomotion No. 1*'s steam.

On 1 July 1828 – almost three years after the line opened – Driver John Cree arrived at the Aycliffe Lane road-crossing.

By one of those spooky quirks of fate it was the very spot where *Locomotion No. 1* had first been lowered onto the Stockton to Darlington line. John began to take on water, so he was almost certainly not standing at the controls behind the boiler. The driver didn't want that precious steam blowing out of the valve while he waited for the tank to fill. He did what many experienced drivers did.

---

* James Stephenson did stay on as one of the top five drivers, along with John Cree.

He tied down the safety valve.

John waited with his water pumper, Edward Turnbull, till he judged there'd be enough pressure in the boiler. He waited too long. The gurgling and hissing of the water would have warned him that a disaster was imminent. He had a choice – untie that valve or run for it. If he ran then *Locomotion* would explode … and locomotives were expensive to replace.

> 'Explosions are not comfortable.'
>
> *Yevgeny Zamyatin (1884–1937), Russian sci-fi writer* *****

We can imagine him trying to untie that valve. Maybe the knot was too tight. Maybe his fingers became thumbs in the panic. Whatever happened, he must have known his fate a split second before it hit him.

I imagine his last words were, 'Oh, b—'

Stephenson's engineer, Timothy Hackworth, said in his diary …

> 'July 1st, 1828, John Cree, going down the line, No 1 locomotive at Aycliffe Lane, while getting water, the engine exploded near one o'clock. He died on the 3rd at 3 o'clock morning.'

What EXACTLY happens when a boiler explodes? Timothy Hackworth doesn't record the injuries – he'd have seen the results of a boiler explosion a few times and wouldn't WANT to record the horrific effects.

However, a doctor can tell us the scenario …

---

* And master of stating the bleedin' obvious.

DANGEROUS DAYS DEATH II

STEAM BOILER EXPLOSION

Victim: John Cree

The steam boiler explodes, and the blast wave hurtles towards you at close to the speed of sound, around 768 miles per hour – there is no escape. The hot steam hits you full in the chest like a charging elephant, turning your lungs into a bloody mush and forcing the air from your chest into your large blood vessels. As the energy of the blast hits your ear drums, it bursts them in an instant.

Lower down, in the depths of your belly, your bowels and stomach burst open, their contents spilling into your abdomen, today's breakfast mixing with yesterday's waste.

Of course, being steam, it is also extremely hot so any exposed skin, such as the hands and face, gets cooked at the same time.

As the actual force of the blast hits your body, it throws you backwards and you can't escape the pieces of boiler shrapnel that penetrate your body. You are the focus of a blind, deranged circus knife-thrower. Luckily, you are dead at this point.

Dr Peter Fox

John Cree survived over two days before he died. Other drivers must have died more quickly, in the way Dr Peter Fox described.

'The life of the dead is placed in the memory of the living.'

Marcus Tullius Cicero (106–43 BC), Roman philosopher

Sadly very few histories place John Cree's sacrifice in the memory of the living. If the accident is mentioned the reports simply say 'The driver was killed'.

It makes you want to argue, 'That driver had a name, a life, a family, and deserves to be remembered as John Cree, not as the anonymous "driver".'

'The dead cannot cry out for justice. It is a duty of the living to do so for them.'

Lois McMaster Bujold (1949—), American sci-fi writer

Locomotion terminus

Locomotion No. 1 was rebuilt and ran again until 1841. Then it ended its days with the wheels removed and used as a stationary pumping engine.* In 1857 it was rescued and preserved. From 1892 to 1975 the old locomotive was put on display on one of the platforms at Darlington's main station, Bank Top.

And what, you may ask, happened to hapless water pumper Edward Turnbull? Ed was scalded by the steam, but survived with a face that was stained and scarred with black speckles by the accident. Maybe he just ran faster than Driver Cree. When he returned to work he was known to his workmates as 'Spotty Turnbull'.

---

* Not a lot of sentiment there then. It sounds a rather undignified fall from grace for such an historic machine. But Trevithick's pioneering locomotive was very quickly shifted to duties as a steam hammer.

Cruel … but probably better than being known as 'The late Edward Turnbull'.

Did you know … high horse

Horses and trains operated on the Stockton and Darlington Railway for many years. On the downhill stretches the horses had been unhitched and had to gallop behind the train. But it exhausted the horse. So a special cart was built so the horse could ride in comfort, chewing its food. The horses loved it. The *Liverpool Mercury* reported: 'He gallops up and jumps into it at full speed and can be got out again and attached again without stopping.' The horse seemed to know the effort it was being spared.

⌒ STEPHENSON'S FAME ⌒

George Stephenson became one of the heroes of the Industrial Revolution. He is up there with the Father of Steam Power, James Watt. An English novelist wrote:

'To us, the moment 8.17 a.m. means something – something very important, if it happens to be the starting time of our daily train. To our ancestors, such an odd eccentric instant was without significance – did not even exist. In inventing the locomotive, Watt and Stephenson were part inventors of time.'

Aldous Huxley (1894–1963)

Geordie Stephenson's success with the Stockton and Darlington Railway led to him establishing his company as the major builder of steam locomotives on railways in the United Kingdom, United States and much of Europe.

The Pease family came up with the idea of a railway line from the coalfields of Durham to the port at Stockton. Stephenson did not get all the credit at the time. The *Observer* wrote in 1830 …

> 'The adaptation of the railways to speed was never, we believe, thought of till the opening of the celebrated Stockton & Darlington rail-road, a work which will forever reflect honour on its authors, for the new and striking manner in which it practically demonstrated all the advantages of the invention.'
>
> Observer, *April 1830*

The 'authors' were the company, not the engineer. The *Observer* forgot that Pease's company envisaged a horse-drawn tramway. Stephenson's great contribution – his 'genius' – was to bring steam engines and railway lines together.

> 'Talent hits a target no one else can hit; Genius hits a target no one else can see.'
>
> *Arthur Schopenhauer (1788–1860), German philosopher*

George Stephenson. Talent or genius?

TEN WAYS TO BE BLOWN UP

'All men make mistakes, but only wise men learn from their mistakes.'

Winston Churchill (1874–1965), British politician and historian

Who do you think you are kidding Mr Churchill? When railway workers made mistakes they often didn't have a chance to learn from them. They were too dead. The wise workers learned from other people's mistakes.*

A steam locomotive is a metal firebox inside a boiler full of water. The steam it produces makes the pistons move. Too much steam and the safety valve opens. Simple. In theory. So how come so many exploded?

- ⚙ The firebox can collapse with the heat, usually when the operator lets the water get too low or fastens down the safety valve for speed – human error.

- ⚙ The boiler can blow outwards with the pressure, especially if the safety valve doesn't work – faulty design.

- ⚙ The boiler or firebox can corrode and become weak with age and needs replacing before it cracks open – faulty maintenance.

There have been many locomotive boiler explosions down the years. If we wish to be 'wise' and avoid being a victim we can learn from past mistakes.

---

* Pop singer Jim Morrison once said, 'Some of my greatest mistakes have been haircuts.' As he was fond of drink and drugs and died aged 27 perhaps he would like to revise that opinion?

1   Newbottle Wagonway, County Durham, 31 July 1815

16 killed (some say 13) and 57 hurt.

The first major railway tragedy and still the worst ever boiler disaster. Before *Locomotion No. 1* was even a twinkle in Geordie Stephenson's eye, William Brunton had designed a 'Steam Horse' with legs that pushed it along. As inquisitive onlookers gathered by the engine the cast-iron boiler exploded. The driver was killed instantly (they usually were) while Brunton's nearby cottage was shattered. Mrs Brunton survived. Most victims were nosy neighbours.

The problem? Probably not enough water in the boiler.

2   Bromsgrove Station, 10 November 1840

2 killed.

Thomas Scaife and Joseph Rutherford of the Birmingham and Gloucester Railway died when an engine boiler exploded.

A mason was employed to create their gravestones. Unfortunately he drew a 4-2-0 locomotive rather than the correct locomotive, which was a 2-2-0. The killer locomotive was ironically named *Surprise*. The loco was for sale at the time of the explosion and on a test run to show how well it could perform.* Scaife was killed instantly but Rutherford survived till the following day.

The headstone of Scaife has the famous poem – copied from an earlier headstone at Whickham, County Durham, for driver Oswald Gardner, killed by a broken connecting

---

* We don't know if it passed the test. But we can have a good guess.

rod. Scaife's headstone says it was composed by 'an unknown friend' but the gravestone is telling lies. It was originally composed by an unknown friend of Oswald Gardner and left on the platform at Blaydon Station.

> 'My engine now is cold and still,
> No water does my boiler fill;
> No coke affords its flame no more
> My days of usefulness are o'er.
> My wheels deny their noted speed,
> No more my guiding hand they heed.
> My whistle, too, has lost its tone.
> Its shrill and thrilling sounds are gone.
> My valves are now thrown open wide
> My flanges all refuse to guide.
> My clacks, also, though once so strong
> Refuse to aid the busy throng.
> No more I feel each urging breath,
> My steam is now condensed in death.
> Life's railway's o'er each station past
> In death I'm stopp'd, at rest at last.
> Farewell, dear friends and cease to weep,
> In Christ I'm safe, in Him I sleep.' ✱

✱ As comedian Spike Milligan wrote in his novel *Puckoon*: 'Not Dead, just Sleeping? He's not kidding anyone but himself.'

3   Miles Platting locomotive shed, Manchester, 28 January 1845

3 killed.

A locomotive called *Irk** was in the shed, getting up steam. Witnesses say it exploded with a force like an earthquake. The blast threw three men over a nearby locomotive. The *Irk* loco flew up after them and settled, upside down, on driver George Mills. A nearby engine cleaner was scalded by the steam and burned by the hot cinders from the firebox but survived. The *Irk*'s safety valves probably failed. Irksome.

4   Wolverton, 26 March 1850

0 killed.

> 'One may have a blazing hearth in one's soul and yet no one ever came to sit by it. Passers-by see only a wisp of smoke from the chimney and continue on their way.'
>
> *Vincent van Gogh (1853–90), Dutch painter*

Sometimes there is a sort of rough justice in the choice of explosion victims. Engine 157 was left on a siding to build up steam. When the steam was up to pressure it started to escape through the safety valve … safely. But the squealing steam started to annoy a fitter's mate who was working alongside the locomotive. He screwed down the safety valves as tightly as he could.

---

* In case you are wondering, the Irk is a river that flows through the north of Manchester. And even if you *weren't* wondering, then the Irk is *still* a river that flows through the north of Manchester.

Of course the pressure rose dangerously. You can guess what happens next. When the driver of 157 arrived the boiler exploded. The main victim was NOT the driver but the fitter's mate who'd screwed the safety valve down. As well as being scalded he had his ear blown off.

Looking on the bright side; at least no one else suffered for his stupidity … and the fitter's mate, like Van Gogh, would be only half as bothered by hissing steam in future.*

5   Longsight, Manchester, 6 March 1853
6 killed.

> 'Where there is mystery, it is generally suspected
> there must also be evil.'
>
> *Lord Byron (1788–1824), English poet*

Boiler explosions were normally investigated by inspectors. This one was a case for Sherlock Holmes. Whodunnit? The shed staff, who maintained the locomotive? Or the driving crew who drove it?

So, Dr Watson, there is nothing like first-hand evidence:

- The old locomotive was in its shed, steaming away, when it exploded and literally blew the roof off the shed.

- There were two safety valves – one on the dome on top of the boiler and one above the firebox. The dome valve was found screwed down, the firebox valve was never found.

- A shed worker said, 'The driver screwed the valves down.' The driver was too dead to defend himself.

---

* But he'd suffer the jokes like: A driver walked into a bar and offered the fitter a whisky. The fitter replied, 'No, it's okay, I've got one ear.'

Open-and-shut case? Except …

➤ The engine firebox was almost rusted away. It had never been replaced in 13 years. Were the shed staff to blame for incompetent maintenance work? If so …

➤ How come the dome valve was screwed down?

➤ Did the shed staff find the dome valve and screw it down BEFORE they handed it to the inspector, then blame the dead driver?

The inspector wasn't fooled and the driver was exonerated … which was no consolation to him at all. A conspiracy to blame a dead man? Don't be surprised.

> 'There is nothing new under the sun. It has all been done before.'
>
> *Sherlock Holmes, English detective in* A Study in Scarlet **✱**

6 Brighton, 17 March 1853

I killed.

The driver of tank engine No. 10 was warned. The driver of a nearby engine told him that his engine should run at 80 pounds pressure. The driver of No. 10 screwed down the safety valve till it reached 100 pounds. Of course it exploded.

The roof of the nearby station was mostly demolished and the driver was probably totally demolished. Why would he do such a thing? Witnesses say the driver had climbed onto

---

✱ Some may wish to add 'fictional detective'. But then some people would claim that God is fictional.

the boiler to heat a can of coffee over the steam … the higher the pressure the hotter the coffee. What price hot coffee?*****

7   Sough, Bolton, 19 January 1857

2 killed.

In the end it all comes down to luck. When locomotive 129 blew up, the fireman was underneath the engine, between the rails, raking out ashes. The exploding boiler threw the train and its six wagons along the line. He was looking at clouds of ashes one second, a cloudy sky the next. He survived, unhurt. His driver and train guard didn't. Luck.**†**

8   Sharp, Stewart & Co. Works, Manchester, 8 October 1858

8 killed … probably.

> 'As the fragments of the bodies were gathered up in sacks there may be a doubt about the seventh. Several of the bodies will be difficult of identification from the shocking manner in which they have been torn to fragments.'
>
> The Hobart Town Daily Mercury – *9 October 1858*

A new locomotive was built and being tested for the Russian railways. When it exploded three boilermakers were killed. A clerk in an office six metres from the explosion survived.

---

* I could say it 'Costa' lot – but I won't.
† Luck is a strange phenomenon. A man who always won at cards always lost at the races. He explained it by saying they wouldn't let him shuffle the horses.

So did a young apprentice who had been sent off to get a new tool from the shed next door. Lucky boy.

As the apprentice looked at the scene of devastation he found body parts scattered around. These included a set of false teeth and a boot with a foot in it. Boilermaker James Carmichael was blown 70 metres over a canal, trailing entrails until he smashed into a wall.

> 'The words of a dead man are modified in the guts of the living.'
>
> *W. H. Auden (1907–73), Anglo-American poet*

His remains, stuck to the wall, were unrecognizable. A badly manufactured boiler plate was blamed.

9 Sharp, Stewart & Co. Works, Manchester, 8 October 1858

One of the dead in the same incident …

… the luckiest – OR unluckiest – victim has to be Thomas Forsyth. Tom was hit by the first train to run on the Liverpool to Manchester service in 1829. He had a leg amputated and replaced with a cork one.

He lived almost 30 years until he was present when that Russian locomotive blew up the Manchester works where he was manager. He suffered a deep wound to his forehead through which, it was reported, 'his brains seeped out'. A shard of iron had killed him instantly.

> 'Thomas Forsyth, the well known and highly skilled manager of the works, was among the killed, his head being much shattered by the force of the explosion and his body much scalded.'
>
> *The* Hobart Town Daily Mercury *– 9 October 1858*

10 Colne Station, Lancashire, 5 May 1864

1 killed.

The driver, George Parker, was chatting to his fireman as the steam built in the locomotive boiler. It burst without warning. Parker was thrown against the wheel of a goods wagon. That could have killed him, but it didn't. The blast had already removed his head.

Fireman William Bird got away with a little scalding, and survived. 'If you can keep your head when all about you are losing theirs ...'

One piece of boiler plate was thrown over a quarter of a mile. The safety vale (which wasn't THAT safe) fell through a cottage roof and injured old Mary Hartley in bed.

The boiler plates had been badly corroded. A few days before the accident inspectors said the permitted pressure of 120 psig was too low. The boiler could take 140.

How wrong could they be?

So, almost 40 years after John Cree lost his life in a boiler explosion, railway workers and the public were still in danger. Wise men learn from their mistakes?

Go Forth and die

George Stephenson's railway works at Forth Street in Newcastle made locomotives by hand. There was not even a crane there until 1837. Heavy lifting was done by ropes and pulleys. Accidents were frequent.

George's brother-in-law, Stephen Liddell, and his brother, John, both died there. There was no compensation culture but George stepped in to support both families after the fatal incidents.

Years before, George had risen to a position of authority at Killingworth when he took over the job of the top engineer who died ... in an accident.*

Having lost a baby daughter, seen his father blinded and maimed in an accident, and buried two wives as well as his star S&DR driver and the Forth Street men, George was a dangerous man to know.

And an 11th from the USA ...

There were unfortunate Fourth of July fireworks on the Harlem Railroad in New York, 1839. A derailed locomotive exploded as workers arrived to put it back on the track. The report said ...

> 'The chief engineer was blown to pieces – his legs went into Union Park, his arms on to a pile of lumber on the other side of the avenue, and his head was split in two parts. His abdomen was also burst and his intestines scattered over the road.'

It makes it sound quite a neat dissection with arms together in one place and legs in another.

---

* I'm sure that with a little more research we could weave a conspiracy theory from that 'convenient' death?

CARNIVAL AND CATASTROPHE

> 'We arrived at Bexhill-on-Sea, where I got off.
> It wasn't easy. The train didn't stop there.'
>
> *Spike Milligan*, Adolf Hitler: My Part in His Downfall

— MARKET MANIA —

The 1820s had come in with discussions about horse power versus stationary steam engines versus locomotives. By the end of the decade the locos were winning and the railway revolution was about to explode like a badly built boiler.

The railway revolution was driven by greed, and a desire to make money. But it was also driven by public demand and excitement at the new technology – like e-books today. If the public want the new technology then the money-men will supply it. At a *double* cost ... the cost of the machine, and the cost to the purveyors of the old technology.*

---

* By 2014 over 50 per cent of households will own an e-reader, so there's every chance you'll be reading this on a screen right now. But the cost wasn't just £100. It was the jobs of workers in bookshops. In 2012 over 400 bookshops closed. By 1830 the stagecoach industry was worried. With good right. Those drivers and grooms and innkeepers had a bleak future. Like booksellers today ... or writers. Eeeek!

Canal owners were facing a collapse of their power to exploit the people of Britain. They had been carrying the best part of a million passengers a year. When the trains came along to threaten their wealth they put up a rearguard, spoiling action in the courts and in Parliament. They were always destined to fail, as the immutable laws of progress demanded they should.

> 'Canals superseded to a large extent the means of transport previously employed; if railroads are found better than canals the latter must, in their turn, give way.'
>
> The Times *(1824)* *

The little Stockton and Darlington adventure had sparked the public interest into a forest fire. The 5 per cent dividend it paid to the investors fanned the flames under the crucibles of their hearts of gold.

With respect to the good burgers of Stockton and Darlington, they were small towns. If the railways were going to prove themselves they needed the next step to be bigger and bolder. The town of Manchester had mills rolling out cotton by the ton. The steam-powered mills were merciless masters ...

---

* Note the date. A year before the Stockton and Darlington captured the hearts of the travelling public. Maybe this was written by the resident astrologer?

> 'While the engine runs, the people must work – men, women and children are yoked together with iron and steam. The animal-machine is chained fast to the iron machine, which knows no suffering or weariness.'
>
> *James Phillips Kay (1804–77), British politician, quoted in 1832 report*

Liverpool had a port that landed the raw cotton and could export the finished product.

Liverpool had the dock capacity because its old prime trade export had dwindled to nothing. That trade had been slavery. And slavery was dead, had rung down the curtain and joined the bleedin' choir invisible. This was an ex-trade, but it left stains and shadows on the city.

> 'History is nothing but the soul's old wardrobe.'
>
> *Heinrich Heine (1797–1856), German poet*

Liverpool needed a fresh new trade to go with its fresh new moral stance and fresh new conscience. Cotton.*

So a partnership with Manchester was made in heaven … except the two cities were 35 miles apart. The answer? A railway … with TWO parallel lines to avoid the nose-punching. And steam power to avoid the oat-munching.

---

* 'Yes, all right, so cotton is still picked by slaves, and *yes* it will be for another 30+ years. But that is America's problem, not ours. This is Business. Our hands are clean … because we wash our hands of this inconvenient truth. Yours sincerely, The British Cotton Merchants, importers and manufacturers … on behalf of the British cotton wearers. PS: how much were the workers paid for making *your* smart trainers? Let he who is without sin …'

The Liverpool to Manchester Canal had carried the cotton cargo – slowly and none too reliably.* Slow transport was always prone to pilfering and a dry summer or icy winter meant costly delays. Worst of all it was a monopoly and the owners of the canal could squeeze the carriers for every penny. Liverpool merchant Joseph Sandars led the fightback and had the money to back his vision.

A railway would end the profiteering of the canal owners. Wonderful. Unless you were a profiteer. And a rich profiteer would do his best to wreck the plans of the railway plotters … by fair means or foul … or very foul. After all, all's fair in love and racketeering.

― SANDARS SABOTAGED ―

Joseph Sandars had sent out exploratory teams as early as 1822 and they were targeted for attacks. Sandars' partner was William James, a lawyer and surveyor, who knew the canal owners would be out to stop them·

James was a visionary.

> 'The empires of the future are empires of the mind.'
> *Winston Churchill*

He is one of the forgotten heroes of the railway age. He's been called, 'Father of the Railway System' on a memorial in his home town of Henley-in-Arden.

---

* Francis Berry, a draper from Bath, complained that the value of his clothing depreciated by 20 per cent on their journey as fashions changed while they were in transit. Witty but Berry unlikely.

Did you know ... William James

William James surveyed many lines, at his own ruinous expense, at a time when he was ridiculed. Back in 1802 he proposed a railway at Bolton when steam locomotives were still a dream of Trevithick.

By 1822 he was bankrupted and too ill to profit from his visionary surveys. In his debtor's prison he drafted a plan for a national rail network.

In 1825 George Stephenson used much of William James's Liverpool and Manchester survey but never acknowledged his debt.*

James's Canterbury and Whitstable survey was adopted by Robert Stephenson soon after – at least Robert DID credit James. 'You plan 'em, Will, we'll cash in,' the Stephensons must have chuckled.

It was a stagecoach journey in the winter of 1837 that gave James pneumonia from which he died. Should have stuck to the railways.

William James met opposition from many and unexpected quarters when he tried the first Liverpool and Manchester survey in 1822 ...

➤ He was opposed by landowner Robert Bradshaw and James went in fear of his life. James hired a notorious heavyweight boxer as a bodyguard. The pugilist's job was to carry the theodolite, but he was beaten in a battle and the instrument destroyed.

---

* A 2007 biography of James is subtitled, 'The man who discovered George Stephenson'. Geordie's ghost must have had steam coming out of his eerie ears at that.

> Bradshaw had persuaded the coal miners that a railway line was not in their interest, so the miners marauded and mugged on his behalf. (In fact the railways would benefit the miners enormously.)

> The scared surveyors took to working at night to fool the mercenary miners.* When the miners laid their hands on James they threatened to throw him down a mineshaft. (They didn't carry out the threat.)

> Farmers barred their gates against James and their labourers were armed with shotguns and pitchforks. Theirs were no idle threats like the miners' ones. A chain-man in James's team was run through the back with a pitchfork as he tried to flee.

> In the villages posses of women and children mobbed the surveyors and threw stones, all the while screaming abuse. St Helens was especially violent – ironic as Rainhill is just four miles south of St Helens and the 1829 Rainhill locomotive trials would be greeted with enthusiasm and fascination. Maybe by the time of the trials the people has finally recognized the financial benefits?

> 'Of mankind we may say in general they are fickle, hypocritical, and greedy of gain.'
> *Niccolò Machiavelli (1469–1527), Italian historian, diplomat*

---

* Yes, I too wonder how you survey land at night. As you know surveying is the science of accurately determining the terrestrial or three-dimensional position of points and the distances and angles between them. How can you do that when you can't see the points? Can you see the point?

➤ The surveyors were safe only when they reached Chat Moss, an expanse of bog that lay on the route. The locals left William James to wallow. He almost sank under the sucking ooze.*****

➤ The attacks almost succeeded. The survey was delayed, the delays cost William James time and time is money ... which he lost. He was thrown into jail for bankruptcy.

➤ But the opponents' victory was hollow.

> 'Violence does, in truth, recoil upon the violent, and the schemer falls into the pit which he digs for another.' **†**
>
> *Arthur Conan Doyle (1859–1930), Scottish doctor and writer*

— ROBERT RUNS —

> 'You pointed out to me that attention and obedience to my dear father would afford me music at midnight.'
>
> *Robert Stephenson (1803–59), engineer, letter to William James*

Music at midnight can be a bit discordant and annoying at times. Robert Stephenson paid attention to his father and

---

* Even when the work started opponents spread scare stories of workers, horses and wagons vanishing into the Chat Moss slime. In fact pouring foundation materials into swampy ground was a well-established engineering practice. Bog standard, you might say. Houses close to Parliament were built on mudflats reclaimed that way.

† This is a metaphorical pit, not the pit the miners left to attack the surveyors. Just in case you were confused. You weren't confused? Sorry.

was obedient. But George Stephenson was not an easy man to love and the two had their fallings out.

In 1824 the lure of El Dorado – the fabulous wealth in the mines of South America – seemed to be singing a different music at midnight to Robert. He decided to go and seek his fortune just as Richard Trevithick had ten years before.*

Why did Robert leave at that time? The Stockton and Darlington Railway was close to opening – it could well have *been* open if a foul and wet winter hadn't delayed the track-layers.

Writing about the Mexican offer, Robert said …

> 'What an opening this is for me as an entry into business.'
>
> *Robert Stephenson, letter to his father*

But Robert was just 20 years old and already a managing partner in the booming engineering business in Newcastle. How big an opening did he want? Like Charlie Bucket he'd already found Willy Wonka's golden ticket in the lottery of life. Robert was a Charlie.

Was that tale of seeking an 'opening' just an excuse? A cover for something murkier? The big giveaway was his letter, written in April 1824, to his Liverpool and Manchester Railway friend, William James. Robert said that he'd turned down the Mexico contract and could James give him a job?

A big clue there. Robert wanted another job – *any* job – to escape the Newcastle partnership. Maybe a job on the Liverpool and Manchester Railway project? But George Stephenson got the Liverpool and Manchester survey job.

---

* There was no good news from Trevithick's adventure. Maybe Robert Stephenson should have taken the hint?

Despair. Robert could work for his father in Newcastle … or work for his father in Liverpool.

He chose Mexico. Robert told his worried Newcastle engineering partners he'd be gone for a year. He had signed a contract for three years. Deceitful.

— GEORGE STEPS IN —

'Success has always been a great liar.'

Friedrich Nietzsche (1844–1900), German philosopher

William James emerged from debtor's prison cell to take up the reins of the Liverpool and Manchester project. But, in one of those cruel twists of fate, James was dumped by the Liverpool and Manchester board.* And the *really* bad news? Lead investor Joseph Sandars told William James …

'We have engaged your friend, Mr G. Stephenson.
I regret that by delay you have lost the confidence
of the investors.'

Joseph Sandars, letter to William James

Delay? *Delay?* The poor bloke had been in prison. William James must have been distraught – especially when Sandars

---

* Yes, that's right. The L&M asked him to survey the line through (literally) sticks and stones, not to mention pitchforks and guns. His own businesses went bankrupt as he battled to achieve the investors' dream … and they sacked him. Loyalty? Sentiment? The railway builders had no conscience. Frailty, thy name is railway investor.

said he wanted Stephenson to use James's plans. Sandars added,

'I am sure the appointment of Stephenson will be agreeable to you.'

As agreeable as a bacon sandwich to a vegan. Some people may have replied with a string of expletives. Certainly the word 'duplicity' featured in James's hurt reaction. He refused to hand over the plans. (Wouldn't you?)

William James wrote to his brother-in-law, Paul Padley, for help in the matter. Paul had been his right-hand man on the survey. Back-stabbing bruv Paul replied …

'I have accepted an offer made to me by Mr Geo. Stephenson of becoming one of his surveyors.'

Paul Padley, of course, had William's plans. There is such a thing as kicking a man when he's down. This was kicking him then running a train over him.

William James's only consolation was a commission to engineer a new Canterbury and Whitstable railway line. It could restore his fortunes. But Canterbury and Whitstable sacked him too. They couldn't replace him with Mr Geo. Stephenson, could they? Oh yes they could – and did.

When Julius Caesar was stabbed the assassins stabbed one another in their eagerness to plant a knife in his ribs. William James must have known how Caesar felt. He sensed a conspiracy and wrote …

'I conclude that Stephenson's intrigues are still predominant in Canterbury.'

Good old Geordie Stephenson. The father of all assassins?

When William James was arrested for debt his 'friend' Robert Stephenson must have felt the guilt that George clearly didn't.*****

In 1824 George Stephenson's second survey was subject to the same hostile, bullying tactics from the canal owners. After the local enthusiasm that was buoying George through Stockton and Darlington surveys, the Liverpool and Manchester experience must have given him a sinking feeling. It would prove a chastening experience for Geordie.

◎ Robert Stephenson was the literate and numerate partner in the father-and-son team, but he had sailed off to South America. George was left with some barely competent assistants.

◎ The opponents tried a new dirty tricks campaign that argued: 'Locomotives explode. Let the barge stay in charge.' Stephenson retaliated with his own dirty tricks, producing a pamphlet that suggested canal mogul, Lord Sefton (the greatest landowner on the route), approved of the railway.

◎ Stephenson's surveyors tried to work at night. The objectors rumbled them and fired shots in the air to scare the plotters off. They had threatened to throw James down a mineshaft. They threatened to throw Geordie Stephenson into a pond.

---

* Another clue. Years later, when the Stephensons were riding high on their engineering fortune there was an appeal made to support the impoverished William James. Robert subscribed. George refused ... and was furious with his son for supporting James. Magnanimous in victory? Geo. couldn't even spell it ... no, really.

The delaying tactics had ruined William James financially. Now they would succeed in ruining Stephenson's plans. In the rush to present his survey to Parliament he relied on apprentices to make the vital measurements he should have carried out himself. If the calculations were wrong then the whole survey would be flawed. They were wrong.

— PARLIAMENTARY PAIN —

'Literacy is a bridge from misery to hope. It is a tool for daily life in modern society. Literacy is the road to human progress and the means through which every man, woman and child can realize his or her full potential.'

Kofi Annan (1938—), Ghanaian diplomat
Secretary-General of the United Nations 1997–2006

Geordie didn't learn to read till he was 19 and was never fluent.* It was a handicap that probably cost him the initial contract on the Liverpool and Manchester Railway scheme.

1825 was the first of George Stephenson's finest hours when the S&DR opened to adoring public.

1825 was the worst of hours when he was humiliated over the Liverpool and Manchester survey fiasco.

---

* There is a theory that he was dyslexic. As William Archibald Spooner (1844–1930) may have agreed that sort of difficulty would have been a blushing crow to a lesser man.

When George was challenged by Parliament to present his plans in 1825 he made a pig's ear of it. He was underprepared and misinformed by those incompetent assistants. Opposition barrister, Edward Hall Alderson,* made mincemeat of the pig's ear.

'How wide is the River Irwell at the point where the railway crosses it, Mr Stephenson?'

Mr Stephenson didn't know.

Geordie hit bottom when Alderson dismissed his erroneous evidence as a demonstration of 'how utterly and totally devoid he is of common sense'. Ouch.†

The project was rejected by Parliament and scapegoat Geordie was sacked. He went home to finish the Stockton and Darlington Railway and lick his wounds.‡

> 'I don't measure a man's success by how high he climbs but by how high he bounces when he hits bottom.'
>
> *George S. Patton (1885–1945), WW2 general US Army*

---

* When clever Alderson became a judge he conducted a trial to determine who had won the 1844 Derby. He demanded the winner, Running Rein, be produced in court. When it failed to answer the summons it was disqualified. The judge must have wanted to hear evidence straight from the horse's mouth.

† Sore loser Stephenson would go on to claim the misinformation came from saboteur surveyors planted by canal-owing rivals. But one of the surveyors, Hugh Steele, took the failure so much to heart he committed suicide.

‡ For once the proud Geordie didn't try to bluster and blame his way out. 'I was not long in the witness box before I began to wish for a hole to creep out at,' he confessed. Stephenson's tormentor, Posh People's Hero Alderson,. was knighted in 1830. Poor People's Hero Stephenson repeatedly declined a knighthood.

— STEPHENSON'S BOUNCE —

George Stephenson was in disgrace in Lancashire. His replacements were engineers George and John Rennie, while the new surveyor was Irishman Charles Vignoles. Perhaps he'd kissed the Blarney Stone, because he was far more eloquent in promoting his scheme.

> 'If one could only teach the English how to talk, and the Irish how to listen, society here would be quite civilized.'
>
> *Oscar Wilde (1854–1900), Irish writer and poet*

Vignoles' new tactics? Appeal to the canal owners' pockets. They were offered shares in the railway company. Many refused, some accepted and that was all that was needed … the enemy camp was divided.* The bill went back to Parliament and was passed in May 1826. It would allow Vignoles' survey, and Sandars' financial package, to go ahead.

Now the question was who would get the job of building the railway? It was a two-horse race. (Two horses, three jockeys some pedants may argue.)

Horse 1: John and George Rennie – who had helped Vignoles push the plan through Parliament.

Horse 2: George Stephenson – who had just had a sensational success with the Stockton and Darlington Railway.

The Rennies made a huge tactical error. They said they would build the line so long as George Stephenson was

---

* The money-grubbing Bradshaw rather cheekily suggested he would accept … if he could have 100 per cent of the shares. It was probably an expression of his contempt rather than a serious expectation.

excluded. (This is like a footballer saying, 'I'll captain your team so long as the nation's favourite player is dropped.')

The job was handed to George Stephenson. A year after his humiliation in Parliament the man was back. If success is the best revenge, then he was back with a vengeance.

Climb every mountain

'Here's to the crazy ones. The misfits. The rebels. The troublemakers. The round pegs in the square holes. The ones who see things differently. They're not fond of rules. And they have no respect for the status quo. You can quote them, disagree with them, glorify or vilify them. About the only thing you can't do is ignore them. Because they change things. They push the human race forward. And while some may see them as the crazy ones, we see genius. Because the people who are crazy enough to think they can change the world, are the ones who do.'

Steve Jobs (1955–2011), American entrepreneur

George Stephenson and the Prodigal Son Robert set about the daunting task of building a 35-mile line over rivers and through hills and over Lancashire's answer to Grimpen Mire … the evil swamp known as Chat Moss.

'Impossible!' the detractors cried. Stephenson sank wooden hurdles under tons of stone and created a platform for his rails that is still used today. The modern locomotives weigh more than 20 times the early locos and they don't vanish into the sea of black sludge … but stand near the track as one crosses and you can still feel the earth move.

Sixty-three bridges were built of masonry and one of cast

iron. That iron idea would return to haunt Robert Stephenson in years to come.

And still the debate rumbled on. Should the line use locomotives or stationary engines and cable-haulage? Could steam be relied upon as horses could? After all, horses had ruled the rails for a hundred years … at the end of their useful lives they could be recycled into cat-food and didn't explode.

The best way to test the reliability of these new-fangled machines, the money-men decided, was to have a contest. Who would be king of the railroad? Who had the rex-factor? The Rainhill Trials were to be held in October 1829.

Trials and tribulations

'These are the times in which a genius would wish to live. It is not in the still calm of life that great characters are formed. The habits of a vigorous mind are formed in contending with difficulties. Great necessities call out great virtues.'

Abigail Adams (1744–1818), wife and mother to US presidents

George Stephenson had been the go-to man for steam locomotives. But it was son Robert who had been his most effective engineer. When Robert sailed off to Columbia in 1824 the Stephensons' engine works had suffered.

☼ *Locomotion No. 1* broke a wheel within days of the celebrated launch. It took two weeks to find a replacement.

☼ *Locomotion*'s sister engine, *Hope*, was delivered late and so badly built the engineers had to work a fortnight just to make her run at all. Even then she was under-powered. Hope-less, in fact.

☼ Stephenson Senior placed a man called Harrison in charge of the Newcastle works but he didn't last long. A letter to Stephenson Junior moaned he was needed back in Newcastle because Harrison 'killed himself with drinking very speedily'.

☼ Within a year of the Stockton and Darlington line opening the Newcastle engine company was 'distressingly in want of money'. Like *Locomotion* it seemed the wheels were coming off for Stephenson. Did he care? He was off in Liverpool surveying the next big thing. Robert was sorely missed.

Robert returned like a knight errant to rescue the locomotive business in time to equip the Liverpool and Manchester Railway. Still, awarding the locomotive contract to the Stephensons' works was far from certain. There would be serious competition ...

— TIMOTHY HACKWORTH —
(1786–1850)

The competition was announced. The runners and riders rushed to the start line. One of the most interesting runners – and one of the most competent – was Timothy Hackworth. Timothy who?

➤ Tim was a nice lad – the sort you'd want your daughter to marry. He was of a religious bent and refused to work on a Sunday. Under that bald domed head was a steam-powered brain, behind those righteous eyes a fierce work ethic and from the humourless mouth you feel few jests escaped.

➤ Tim was born in Wylam in 1786, where George Stephenson had been born five years before. By 1811 he was building steam locomotives. His biographer would go on to claim …

> 'To him [Hackworth], more than any other man, was due the successful emergence of the locomotive from its unpromising beginnings to a state of wonderful efficiency.'
>
> *Robert Young,* Timothy Hackworth and the Locomotive *(1923)*

➤ Hackworth's fellow engineer was Jonathan Foster, who worked on the steam engines on a Saturday afternoon when the Wylam Colliery shut down. Jon Foster was a chatty bloke who liked to discuss his work. An old Wylam acquaintance turned up each Saturday to listen to rent-a-mouth Foster. An acquaintance who now worked for a rival colliery. A spy who would steal Hackworth and Foster and Hedley's best ideas. No wonder Hedley learned to loathe the spy.

> 'It is only the wise general who will use the highest intelligence for the purposes of spying, and thereby they achieve great results.'
>
> *Sun Tzu (544–496 BC), Chinese military strategist*

➤ The spy's name, the 'old Wylam acquaintance'? You must have guessed, Monsieur Poirot, he was called George Stephenson. Hackworth's Wylam was running steam locos in 1813. Stephenson's Killingworth started in 1814.

➤ Timothy was a man of principle. And one of his principles was to observe the Bible and never work on a

Sunday. The Wylam mine closed on a Sunday, so that was the day for testing the locomotives. As Tim set off to preach one Sunday in 1815 he met one of the Wylam labourers. The conversation went …

LABOURER: Where are you going?*
HACKWORTH: I am going to preach.
LABOURER: Are you not going to do your work?
HACKWORTH: I have other work to do today.
LABOURER: Well if you won't work someone else will and you'll lose your job.
HACKWORTH: Lose or not lose. I shall not break the Sabbath.

Tim was sacked

➤ In 1824 Timothy Hackworth took Robert Stephenson's place in the Stephenson factory in Newcastle. He was called a 'borrowed man'. It was Timothy's skill and persistence that got them to work at all. Without Timothy Hackworth the Stockton and Darlington Railway could have been pulled by good old Dobbin. The whole railway revolution could have stalled had it not been for terrific Tim.

'There are two kinds of people, those who do the work and those who take the credit. Try to be in the first group; there is less competition there.'
    Indira Gandhi (1917–84), Indian Prime Minister †

---

* Translated from the Geordie tongue for the convenience of more genteel readers. The original read, 'Where's thee gannin?' See what I mean?
† You have to take this lady seriously. The day before she was assassinated she made a speech in which she said, 'I am alive today, I may not be there tomorrow.' How prescient is that? Or you could argue that, as she was shot by her own bodyguards, her judgement wasn't that prophetic.

➤ Tim made a major breakthrough – aligning the steam blast pipe in locomotives. In 1827 his *Royal George* locomotive was the most efficient engine of the time. Again, you don't need to be Gypsy Rose to read the future in the teabags. Yes, the Stephensons 'borrowed' the idea from their borrowed man and won everlasting fame with their *Rocket* locomotive.

> 'An idea needs propagation as much as a plant needs watering. Otherwise both will wither and die.'
>
> *B. R. Ambedkar (1891–1956), Indian politician and philosopher*

Oh, Timothy, you needed a good agent.

➤ The subtle Stephenson recognized Tim's talents and in 1824 made Timothy a new offer – the post of manager on the imminent Stockton and Darlington Railway. Tim settled in the locomotive headquarters in Shildon, and slaved harder than his labourers to keep the Stockton and Darlington Railway running. As an old workman said …

> 'Mr Hackworth worked in weather frosty enough to freeze the tallow as it ran down the candle sides.'
>
> *Quoted in the* Northern Echo *(1872)*

➤ When it came to entering the Rainhill Trials, Timothy Hackworth was a natural contender and a favourite to win. If you'd been a bookie you'd have stopped taking bets on him.

> 'Timothy Hackworth is original, is of himself improving the locomotive in essentials as no other man is doing and is incomparably in advance of George Stephenson in everything. He has, and is, stamping a character upon the structure of the locomotive of the very highest importance.'
>
> *From* The World's Railway
> *by J. G. Pangborn (1844–1914), historian*

➤ He remained with the Stockton and Darlington for 15 years as his boss George travelled the country making his fortune. Dim Tim.

BRIEF TIMELINE – THE TWENTIES

1821   Parliament grants Pease his plan for a Darlington to Stockton railway. Michael Faraday has demonstrated an electric motor in London but a bigger shock is the death of poet John Keats in Rome from tuberculosis at the age of 25. There lies one whose name was writ in water.

1823   Charles Macintosh makes waterproof fabric for coats and the 'Mac' is born. Where will he make them? Damp Manchester, where better?

1825   The first train runs from Darlington to Stockton pulled by *Locomotion No. 1*. Sixty banks are forced to close due to disastrous speculation in foreign companies. Maybe safer to invest in Brit schemes … railways perhaps? Betting scandal gets bookies banned from Lord's Cricket Ground.*

---

* Late-running trains? A credit crunch caused by rash bank speculation? Betting scams? Yes, this is 1825, not 2014.

1826   George Stephenson engaged to build the Liverpool
        and Manchester Railway line. Lancashire
        hand-loom workers smash a thousand new steam-
        powered looms. In Stockton chemist John Walker
        invents the friction match while James Sharp in
        Northampton installs the first domestic gas cooker.

1828   *Locomotion No. 1* explodes with fatal results. No
        one really discouraged.* Suffolk squire, William
        Corder, the Red Barn Murderer, is hanged (slowly
        and publicly) and Victorian theatre's most popular
        melodrama is born.† In Edinburgh Burke and
        Hare are caught and tried for killing and selling
        corpses to anatomists for experiment. The Duke
        of Wellington, hero of Waterloo, becomes Prime
        Minister.

1829   Trials are held at Rainhill near Liverpool to
        decide the best locomotives to pull the Liverpool
        to Manchester trains. Stephenson's *Rocket* wins.
        Robert Peel sets up the first police force, too late to
        arrest the Prime Minister, Duke of Wellington, for
        his duel with the Earl of Winchelsea.‡

---

* James Watt may have ranted, 'I told you so. High pressure steam is dangerous.' But since he died in 1819 no one was listening.
† For additional entertainment and public pleasure the hanging rope is sold for a guinea an inch. It'll look nice on your mantelpiece.
‡ It was a squabble over politics and religion. Wellington fired first … and missed. He SAID he had missed on purpose, but he was well known for being a rotten shot. We'll never know the truth. Winchelsea fired and missed, he apologized and honour was satisfied. Winchelsea's apology had been prepared in advance so we can be pretty sure his claim to have missed deliberately can be believed.

1830   In September the Liverpool and Manchester
        Railway opens with huge fanfare and a death. Also
        the death of King George IV. William IV becomes
        king. The Kent agricultural workers are rioting
        now – they follow the mythical 'Captain Swing'.
        Wellington is resisting reform so the cities rise in
        riots too and he gets the boot.

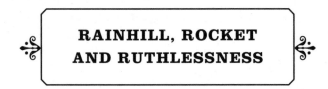

RAINHILL, ROCKET AND RUTHLESSNESS

> 'George Stephenson's *Rocket* had a glorious youth,
> a humiliating middle life and an honoured and
> eternal old age.'
>
> From George Stephenson *by Ada Louise Barrett (1849–83)*

Rocket's 'glorious youth' included great gouts of blood on its
wheels. But, like terrorists who become revered members of
the establishment, the blood is washed from the memory.

The Rainhill Trials were not just a test to see who would
build the locomotives for the line. They were also a challenge
between the moving loco and the stationary engine … so there
were doomsayers who wanted ALL of the entrants to fail.

It was also a sneaky piece of free publicity. There's nothing
like a good race to pique the interest of the public. And the
Rainhill Trials were nothing like a good race.

— THE ENTRANTS —

Cyclopede

It was worked by a horse tramping along a treadmill. It didn't
get far before the horses had to stop for hay. The horse fell
through the belt but the machine would be disqualified
anyway as the rules specified a steam locomotive.* Some
historians think the *Cyclopede* was designed as a joke to
entertain the crowds. The *Cyclopede* withdrew. Then there
were four …

Novelty

Novelty's builders heard about the contest just seven weeks
before it happened and cobbled together a machine from
bits of London fire-engines. It was described as a 'tea urn' by
a witness. Built by Braithwaite and Ericsson (a Swedish army
captain) it was soon the favourite as it sped along at 30 miles
per hour.† It hadn't been properly tested – there were no rails
in London. On its first run it had problems with the wheels.
Timothy Hackworth generously offered to repair the fault,
and he personally took out the broken segment, welded it,

---

* One of the side-shows was a machine named Winan's Manumotive
Carriage powered by two men pushing a geared lever (like a modern
'cross-trainer'). The L&M directors liked it so much they ordered 12
but there's no record of them ever being used. There was a sarcastic
suggestion that any passengers who helped out with the pushing should
get a discount.

† At one stage *Novelty* overtook Stephenson's *Rocket*. A witness said, 'I
shall never forget the expression on Robert Stephenson's face.' We can
imagine Robbie's face did not say, 'Oh, jolly well done, you chaps.'

and put it back in position with his own hands.***** Its bellows burst and repeated boiler failures led to its withdrawal. Two down, three to go …

The *Perseverance*

It didn't. It was built in Edinburgh by Timothy Burstall who made steam coaches. A cheeky Scottish assistant had wandered into the Stephensons' works in Newcastle asking about the locomotives before he was questioned and turfed out. Spying was clearly part of the game. But it did *Perseverance* no good. The striking red wheels were damaged as it was unloaded at Liverpool and never reached a useful speed. They aimed to conquer, but the Scots missed.

> 'I was born in London, and went to school in Scotland – I used to be dead tired when I got home at night.'
>
> *Norman Wisdom (1915–2010), English actor/comedian*

The *Sans Pareil*

Timothy Hackworth's effort. Of course the Stephensons had the resources while Tim had little capital or workshop facilities to work with. The Stephensons didn't pay him a big enough wage to build his own machine. What little money he had was needed to keep his large family of two sons and five daughters fed and educated. He used the last of his father's inheritance to invest in building *Sans Pareil*.

---

* You have to wonder if generous Tim quite grasped the concept behind the word 'com-pet-ition'.

The owners of the Shildon works condescended to allow him to build his new machine there – so long as he continued the full-time job of maintaining their Stockton and Darlington machines. It was like asking Van Gogh to produce a masterpiece with a box of crayons. He worked night and day and had little time to test the loco.

The Stephensons wanted to win. Tim Hackworth *needed* to win.

> 'Desperation is the raw material of drastic change. Only those who can leave behind everything they have ever believed in can hope to escape.'
>
> *William S. Burroughs (1914–97), American novelist*

The expert opinion is that *Sans Pareil would* have won, but for its faulty valves. It was faster, more powerful and more fuel efficient than *Rocket*. But then there was one …

Rocket

The sunflower yellow boiler was topped with a white chimney. Smart as paint.

The Stephensons had taken Hackworth's twin-flue development and improved it. Yet it was Henry Booth – Treasurer to the Liverpool and Manchester Railway – who came up with the most radical improvement: not twin tubes heated in the boiler but 25 small tubes. You don't need to be a professor of maths to know this would increase the heated area and efficiency.* The engine was adapted by Robert

---

* Think of the element in an electric kettle. It has more twists than a Scouts knotting contest.

Stephenson and named … *The Specimen*.* As we all know, *Rocket* won.†

But locomotive power – as opposed to stationary steam engines – won too.

— STEPHENSON SKULDUGGERY —

'Gamesmanship – or the art of winning games without actually cheating.'

Book title, Stephen Potter (1900–69), English author

Robert Stephenson was clearly worried about the competition from Timothy Hackworth. He wrote regular letters to Henry Booth of the L&MR explaining in detail how Hackworth's machine was going to break the rules on emissions and weight. Sneaky.

One letter claimed Hackworth's locomotive was over the four-ton weight limit. The judges disqualified it on this technicality (but allowed it to take part in the trial 'unofficially'). The rules were laid down when the contest was announced. Rules are rules. Nothing suspicious there, you argue. So why (I argue back) was Hackworth not allowed to see the engine being weighed?

---

* Yes, the world's most famous locomotive was almost named after a bottle of a drug-tested athlete's pee. The name changed to echo the American military flare developed in 1812 and called a 'rocket'.

† It had, of course, been entered by Booth, the L&M treasurer, and Stephenson, the L&M chief engineer. What a coincidence. A fix, you say? Perish the thought.

At Rainhill George Stephenson inspected *Sans Pareil* closely and Tim took his old boss for a test run. Geordie asked, 'Timothy, what makes the sparks fly out of the chimney?'

Hackworth touched the exhaust pipe near the cylinders, and explained, 'It is the end of this little fellow that does the business.'

George Stephenson must have choked back the laughter. Hackworth's engine driver spoke for us all when he moaned …

> 'Why did you tell him how you *did* it, sir? He will be trying to fit up the "Rocket" in the same way.'
>
> John Thompson, the driver and Hackworth's foreman at Shildon as told in Practical Mechanics' Journal *(1850)*

Hackworth's reply? He said, 'I don't think so.' On a scale of naïve-to-gullible he was around Planet Cuckoo. The world's greatest judge of steam locomotives. The world's worst judge of his fellow humans?

Driver Thompson decided to guard the *Sans Pareil* all night. He locked himself in the shed containing the engine, but towards daybreak dozed off. When he woke he saw two men getting out of the window of the shed, and he found the chimney door of the *Sans Pareil* open. There were some materials inside the chimney. The secret of the exhaust steam blast had been stolen. The next evening the *Rocket* again appeared; this time she was fitted with a similar device.

The sneaky letters and spying didn't make *Rocket* superior, so maybe the Stephensons tried a more direct form of sabotage? Timothy was short of time so he had outsourced the making of the valves to mate Geordie. At the trials Timothy failed when his locomotive broke down. Geordie won. But it was the *valves* that failed on Timothy's loco. A joint that should have been 7/8 inch was fourteen times thinner at 1/16 inch.

An acquaintance of Hackworth's said later …

> 'I remember Timothy Hackworth showing my father a piece of the broken metal and it was just the thickness of a shilling.'
>
> *Thomas Greener*

The valves were supplied by Robert Stephenson.

Hackworth was furious and wrote to the judges explaining and complaining …

> 'My peculiar situation compelled me to put confidence in others which I found, with sorrow, was but too implicitly placed.'
>
> *Timothy Hackworth*

'Others' is obviously his 'friend' Geordie.

Sans Pareil proved to be a reliable machine. It *was* bought by the Liverpool and Manchester Railway Company and used successfully for 15 years.

People of Shildon still mutter that it was deliberate sabotage. Sour grapes from bad losers?

That's history. The Stephensons had built the line and now they got to build the locomotives. By hook or by crook they had the result they wanted.

— THE GRAND OPENING: —
15 SEPTEMBER 1830

The line was finished. It needed a spectacular opening to show the world the wonders of railways. The builders and their backers got more spectacle than they expected.

> 'The beginnings and endings of all human undertakings are untidy.'
>
> *John Galsworthy (1867–1933), English novelist*

The great day arrived. The world looked on in awe.

There were eight locomotives making the inaugural run to Manchester. The engines, like the exclusive tickets to ride, were colour coded. Only the star guest Duke of Wellington would be pulled by a plain locomotive.*

By their colours ye shall know them.†

Phoenix –	dark green
North Star –	yellow
Comet –	dark red
Rocket –	light blue
Dart –	purple
Meteor –	brown
Arrow –	pink

---

* King George IV was not long dead so Wellington appeared in black out of respect. It wouldn't do to be seen in a pink train would it?

† And by their maker. The eight were all made by George and Robert Stephenson's factory. Two other locomotives were made in London for the L&M Railway but were not invited to take part in the procession. No one was going to steal Master Steam-and-son's thunder that day.

Unlike Stockton and Darlington, this railway had two tracks to reduce the chance of fisticuffed fights over rights of way, barneys, bruisings and batterings. For the opening procession the Duke's train would have one line and the other seven would run on the parallel track.

Robert Stephenson's old boss at Killingworth Colliery said …

> 'The eyes of the whole scientific world were upon the great undertaking.'
>
> *Nicholas Wood, Killingworth Colliery manager (1832)*

Maybe not ALL eyes? Because a cannon was fired as the official starting signal. There wasn't a cannonball in it of course, just wadding material. But that was dangerous enough. The wadding hit a spectator in the face and sent his eyeball rolling down his cheek. Did his wife ask him what he saw at the event? And did he reply, 'I've no eye dear'?

It was not an auspicious start.

The Victim: William Huskisson

> 'I had a mate who was suicidal. He was really depressed, so I pushed him in front of a steam train. He was chuffed to bits.'
>
> *Anonymous*

William Huskisson MP was a victim waiting for his fatal accident.

➤ As a child he broke his arm getting out of bed

➤ Just before he married his horse fell on him

- He was flattened by a carriage at Horse Guards in Whitehall

- He tried to jump a moat of a Scottish castle and snapped tendons in his foot

- After limping back to London he fell off his horse (again) broke his arm (again) before falling out of a carriage and breaking his arm (again)*

- A sore throat never mended and his voice became a rasping hiss

- He headed to France to recover, where (you may be disappointed to learn) he didn't slip on a frog and break his arm. He tripped over a cable and gashed his foot.

- Oh … and he suffered periods of gout.

When 1830 brought the L&MR opening he was sick with a kidney infection that gave him unexpected and awkward urges to pee. He had been given a sick note from his doctors that would excuse him (politely) from accepting invitations.

> 'We are of the opinion that it would be extremely hazardous for Mr Huskisson to undertake a long journey or to incur any abnormal fatigue or exertion for some weeks.'

A hazardous journey? The quacks had been reading the tarot cards.

---

* Arms and carriages and horses. Not surprising he was such an advocate of railways and locomotives.

But the invitation to attend the opening of the L&M was an offer too good to refuse. After all he had been elected Liverpool's Member of Parliament just six years (and three broken arms) before.***** He accepted. He would not be accepting any more thereafter.

Did you know … the forgotten crash

The opening of the Liverpool and Manchester Railway saw the world's first train-on-train crash. One of the coaches pulled by dark-green *Phoenix* lost a wheel. That caused the train to slow. With no signal system in place the following train ran into the back of it. No one was injured, the wheel was reattached and the procession carried on. Omen number 2?

The accident

The colourful parade of trains set off for Manchester as crowds gathered to cheer and wonder. The Duke of Wellington's train, pulled by *Northumbrian*, had the southern track to itself while the other seven trains ran on the northern line. At the halfway point the trains stopped for water.

The passengers were requested not to alight. So what did 50 of them do? They alighted. William Huskisson saw the Duke of Wellington and strolled across to chat to him. The

---

* He won the 1823 election by 236 to 31 … you can see how few people were enfranchised. He'd been re-elected shortly before the opening of the railway. He'd been too poorly to travel to Liverpool and campaign. He just sent a message saying he would cut taxes. He was elected. There's a lesson there for politicians of every coloured rosette you can imagine.

two parliamentarians had had many fallings-out and Huskisson had resigned from Wellington's cabinet the previous year … accidentally.*

Huskisson stood between the rails of the northern line. As the two enemies exchanged polite words someone pointed out (politely) that the light blue *Rocket* was bearing down on that line … out of the blue as it were.

The Austrian ambassador was hauled up into the Duke's carriage. Huskisson panicked. He ran into the path of *Rocket*. He ran back to the Duke's carriage. He grabbed the door and hauled himself up. But the door hadn't been latched. The MP clung to the door as it swung gently into the path of the oncoming train. A pure Keystone Cops moment.

Rocket, like every other locomotive built at that time, had no brakes and driver Joseph Locke applied the usual routine of throwing it into reverse. Too late.

The carriage door was wet from the Lancashire drizzle and Huskisson's fingers slipped. When *Rocket* hit the door he fell backwards and landed between the tracks with his left leg draped across *Rocket*'s line. Huskisson's thigh was crushed.

'It's all over with me. Bring me my wife and let me die,' he gurgled. When his wife arrived she dissolved into hysteria.

> 'Mr. Huskisson's right leg was smashed to mummy.'
>
> Liverpool Albion *newspaper (1830)*

---

* In a row about parliamentary reform Huskisson, a cabinet minister, wrote a stroppy letter to Wellington. Huskisson said that he offered Wellington 'the opportunity of placing my office in other hands'. Wellington took that as a letter of resignation and accepted it. Huskisson said it was NOT meant to be a resignation. Too late. He was relegated to the forsaken and forgotten seats of the back benches.

> 'His leg was squeezed almost to a jelly.'
>
> The Times *(1830)*

'I have met my death,' he whispered. 'God forgive me.' We don't know God's reply.

Eyewitness reports vary. Some say there were 'fiery fountains' of blood spurting from the wound. Others said it just oozed.

A carriage door served as a makeshift stretcher and Huskisson was loaded onto the coach that the band had occupied. The Duke's locomotive was uncoupled and Huskisson rushed to Manchester for medical help. George Stephenson took the controls and reached record speeds … 35 miles per hour and fast … but the MP was slipping faster.*

The end

The doctors decided his situation was so desperate they needed to stop at the first house they came to near the track. It turned out to be a vicarage at Eccles. They slithered over the embankment in a hailstorm and carried the MP inside.

Surgeons from Manchester were asked to attend with their amputation knives and saws. Yet Huskisson had the strength to dictate an amendment to his will.†

As his body was racked with pain he heard distant cannons roar … the Manchester welcome for the Duke of Wellington. The dying man expressed a hope the Duke would be safe.

And that is where he died. The vicarage was perhaps a more appropriate place for God to forgive him.

---

* The waiting crowds cheered manically thinking it was all part of the parade. Their screams drowned Huskisson's.

† He'd discussed updating his will with his secretary only the night before. Spooky.

DANGEROUS DAYS DEATH III

CRUSHING

Victim: William Huskisson

Dr Brandreth reported, 'The leg, half way between the knee and ankle was almost entirely severed. Higher up, between the knee and body, the whole flesh was torn off above the broken bone.' The results, a witness said, were, 'Countenance pale and ghastly, forehead covered with cold perspiration, cold and stiffened extremities, and sickness and oppression in the stomach with frequent convulsive shudders, difficult respiration.'

Crushing results in the skin and underlying muscle being flattened, splitting under the pressure and squashing out either side. Blood vessels burst causing heavy continuous blood loss and leg bones are crushed into the many pieces of an impossible jigsaw. The pain is immense, such that your brain may give in and you lose consciousness. If not then you will watch your blood leaving your leg. With less blood to pump around your body the heart tries harder to get blood everywhere, increasing your pulse. It's a losing battle, more blood is lost, blood pressure falls, you become cold and sweaty. Shock sets in and you feel like you are about to die, which you are. In an attempt to get enough blood to the brain other vital organs are shut down; kidneys fail. Finally a few hours later, no blood is getting to the brain and life leaves you.

Dr Peter Fox

The Duke of Wellington and his sombre fellow travellers arrived at Manchester for a reception and banquet. The weavers and mill workers of the underclasses had their own reception for the man who was denying them the vote and keeping the price of corn too high. They showered Wellington with bricks and vegetables. They cheekily hoisted a French *tricoleur* while Huskisson met his Waterloo.*****
Wellington had said of his own soldiers at Waterloo …

> 'I don't know what effect these men will have upon the enemy, but, by God, they frighten me.'
>
> *Arthur Wellesley (1769–1852) , 1st Duke of Wellington*

He could have echoed that when confronted by the underclasses of Manchester – though they had rotten vegetables, not 24-pounder siege guns.

Wellington refused to travel by train for another 13 years and said sourly, 'The railway will encourage the lower classes to travel about.' Meaning the lower classes should know better and stay in their place. As Wellington said of his own soldiers,

> 'Our army is composed of the scum of the earth – the mere scum of the earth.'

Wellington was right – the railways were a social revolution as well as an economic, technological and industrial revolution. Wellington and his old guard would be swept from power two months later as the scum began to make its voice heard.

---

* The man who had beaten Napoleon was forced to stay in his carriage – defeated by angry weavers. Never mind, the cold meats from the buffet were delivered to him so he didn't go as hungry as the starving rebels.

The L&MR was hailed as the future by some …

'A greater impulse to civilization than it has ever received from any single cause since the printing press first opened the gate of knowledge to the human species.'

The Scotsman *(1830)*

It was berated as a disaster by more conservative voices …

'Poor Huskisson is dead. He has been killed by a steam carriage. The folly of seven hundred people going fifteen miles an hour, in six carriages, exceeds belief. But they have paid a dear price.'

Lord Brougham (1778–1868), UK chancellor *

Running the early railways was not an exact science. Hit and miss … literally at times. As Isambard Brunel's engineer said years later …

'When I look back upon this time it is a marvel to me that we escaped serious accidents. Many times have I taken an engine out, seen a train coming and reversed as quickly as I could. What would be said of such a mode of proceeding now?'

Daniel Gooch (1816–89), Great Western Railway engineer

---

* He also opposed compulsory schooling. Brougham holds the House of Commons record for non-stop speaking at six hours. It would be interesting to know if he said anything intelligent in all that time.

⁓ THE LEGEND THAT LIVES ⁓

Despite the dangers, it seems the Victorian fascination with steam power was undimmed.

> 'I wonder whether, in future ages, men will ever fall down and worship steam engines, as the Caribbeans did Columbus's ships? Why not? Men have worshipped stone men and women; why not line iron? Fancy it!'
>
> *Charles Kingsley (1819–75), English writer*

Yes, Mr Kingsley, and people still worship steam trains.

Huskisson is forgotten for his reforming work. He is famed for being the first railway accident victim but new evidence suggests he was the *second*. At Eaglescliffe, near Stockton, records in the parish state that, in 1827, an unnamed female – thought to be a blind beggar – was 'killed by the steam machine on the railway'.

So Huskisson is famous for something he wasn't, and died of his fame. A woman born three months after Huskisson's death said succinctly …

> Fame is a bee.
> It has a song—*****
> It has a sting—
> Ah, too, it has a wing.
>
> *Emily Dickinson (1830–86), American poet*

---

* Let's face it, Em, a bee may well have a song, but 'Buzz, buzz' is a pretty boring song. Maybe bees just hum their song because they don't know the words?

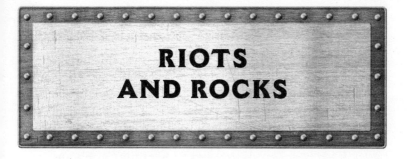

RIOTS AND ROCKS

~ THE IRON AGE ~

'Discontent is the first necessity of progress.'
Thomas A. Edison (1847–1931), American inventor

In 1835 there had been 3,300 stagecoaches carrying 10 million passengers each year. As they raced each other for business they wrecked the roads so road-tolls were increased to pay for the damage and fares went up.

Horses were driven too hard, their lives shortened so horse-costs went up. It was a downward spiral. The railways were the stake through the heart of the ailing stagecoach industry. Dick Turpin would have rued the decline – Black Bess would certainly have celebrated it.

The Liverpool and Manchester Railway was to transform the age. Yet before the construction, before even the survey, it needed a vision. One of the men of vision was Henry Booth, who believed …

'The man of business in Manchester will breakfast at home, proceed to Liverpool by the railways, transact his business, and return to Manchester before dinner.'
Henry Booth, treasurer to the Liverpool and Manchester Railway

When he saw the L&MR opened, and his vision realized, he was sure this was merely the start of something world-changing.

> 'The Golden Age is past and it is to be feared the Iron Age has succeeded. The locomotive engine and railway were reserved for the present day. From west to east and from north to south, the mechanical principle will spread and extend itself. The world has received a new impulse. The genius of the age, like a mighty river of the new world, flows onward, full, rapid and irresistible.'
>
> *Henry Booth (1830)*

Of course the Stephensons were in the driving seat of the railway revolution. Timothy Hackworth, who had made their success possible, went back to working for the Stockton and Darlington Railway. But Geordie and Robert hadn't finished exploiting his genius.

In 1830 Hackworth ordered a new locomotive from the Stephensons' Newcastle works for the Stockton and Darlington line.

The engine, *The Planet*, featured Hackworth's own innovative design: twin, horizontal cylinders operating on crank axles. The Stephensons scoffed at the idea – then delayed completion of their own *Globe* locomotive while they copied *The Planet* drive and used it on the *Globe*. Sneaky.*

> 'We have to distrust each other. It is our only defence against betrayal.'
>
> *Tennessee Williams (1911–83), American playwright*

---

* The *Globe* design was followed by the *Patentee* design which sold around Europe in 1833. It had extra wheels to take a larger boiler. When THAT boiler exploded it killed the driver AND the fireman.

The Stephensons were at the forefront of the expansion of the railways in the 1830s. In 1835 George was appointed chief engineer of the Grand Junction Railway that joined Birmingham to the L&MR. The master did not find it easy to share power with his former pupil, Joseph Locke ... the man who had been on the footplate of *Rocket* when it ran over William Huskisson. The railway directors were so impressed they invited Locke to take sole charge of the building of the line. An outraged Geordie packed his nappies and walked away in 1835.

From then onwards the engineering responsibilities of the company fell onto Robert's shoulders even though George was usually named as 'Engineer-in-Chief'. Robert's shoulders were narrow and the burden heavy.

> 'A king, realizing his incompetence, can either delegate or abdicate his duties.'
> *Marlene Dietrich (1901–92), German-born actress and singer*

Robert persevered with the massive challenge of the London to Birmingham construction. As usual an unsung hero was engaged to do the bulk of the work – this time it was Joseph Locke.

The Stephensons' Newcastle works were continuing to sell locomotives as fast as they could produce them. The third-rate, shoddy locomotives were palmed off onto the Stockton and Darlington Railway ... where Hackworth had the unenviable task of getting them up to speed.*

---

* The duff chuffers were known as 'Jenny Spinners' – barely the power to turn a spinning Jenny wheel, perhaps? Mind you it was Hackworth's son who rubbished the Stephenson locos. He could have been biased. A bit. Or a lot.

Hackworth died in 1850 and we wave goodbye to him from our story. One of life's losers – elbowed to the back of life's race by the Stephensons. His epitaph ... no, not the one actually carved on his grave ... could be:

> 'Hardly any two of Hackworth's engines had been alike. Stephenson on the other hand, when getting hold of a good idea, repeats it over and over again. The result is Stephenson is making lots of money and Hackworth is not; but the latter is compelling locomotive designers all over the world to step right lively to keep up with him.'
>
> *J. Pangborn,* The World's Railway *(1830)*

So Stephenson grew rich. If you judge success in terms of pounds and pence then George Stephenson was a winner and Hackworth a loser. But never forget ...

> 'If you want to know what God thinks of money, just look at the people he gave it to.'
>
> *Dorothy Parker (1893–1967), American author*

BRIEF TIMELINE – THE THIRTIES

1830   The Liverpool and Manchester Railway opens
        with George and Robert Stephenson's locomotives
        and a tragic death.*

1833   At Bagworth, near Leicester, a train collides with
        a horse-drawn cart at a crossing. This leads to
        the invention of the train whistle.† The Grand
        Junction Railway will join Birmingham to the
        L&MR while the London to Birmingham will
        almost link up with it.‡

1835   The London and Birmingham Railway requires a
        tunnel at Watford. It collapses killing ten men. The
        work on the line is not delayed, much to the relief
        in the boardroom of the L&BR Company.

1836   The railway comes to London when the line to
        Greenwich opens.

1837   Princess Victoria comes to the throne and will sit
        there for another 63 years. John Constable dies – he
        has painted Salisbury Cathedral … which must

---

* The death of MP Huskisson was not laid at the doors of the railway
but those of the people of Liverpool. The Reverend Samuel Sanders said
the Liverpudlians had broken the Sabbath, let their evil children run
wild, attended race meetings, got drunk and swore and consorted with
prostitutes. Huskisson had done none of these but he was the sacrificial
goat. Which seems a little unfair. Thank goodness Liverpool today
displays none of those vices or blameless natives like Wayne Rooney
could be rendered as legless as Huskisson.
† The earliest trains had buglers on the roof as the descendants of
stagecoach post-horn players. In the Bagworth case, the system didn't
work. Maybe the horse was deaf.
‡ Passengers had to change stations in Birmingham to travel on to
Liverpool and the north. This was because an ancient landowner refused
permission for the railway to cross his land. The hostile and fractious old
man's name? James Watt. Yes *that* James Watt.

have required some very long ladders and a head for heights. The telegraph is invented to make rail travel safer – between Euston and Camden at first.

1838   Advice to travellers suggests they sit in a coach as far away from the locomotive as possible. In the event of an explosion, the writer advises, 'you may then get away with the loss of just an arm or a leg'. Parliament says train services must carry mail. Five thousand miles of track now. Ocean-going steam-ships pioneered by engineer Isambard Brunel.

1839   Telegraph will run alongside rail tracks. Start of a three-mile tunnel through the Pennines. It will take six years to build and cost well over 30 lives – about a life every 150 metres. Expensive tunnel.

1840   At Farringdon Road, five are injured, one fatally when the driver falls asleep at the controls. It will be another 80 years before a 'Dead Man's Handle' will cure that flaw in the safety systems.

— THE NAVIGATORS —

It was Robert's London to Birmingham line that brought the greatest leap in his renown. One commentator of the time said it was a more impressive feat than the building of the Great Pyramid of Giza.* Workers on the pyramid died for the glory of a pharaoh. Workers on the Birmingham line died for the enrichment of investors and landowners.†

Lefty Bollocks!

---

* And Robert had no mummy to inspire him.
† The line cost £3.5m to build. But £700,000 of that was paid out in compensation to landowners who held the railway builders to ransom.

Speculators risked their money. The workers risked their lives. Those speculators didn't put a lot back into the towns and villages they ploughed through.

'One or two bold speculators had projected streets; and one had built a little, but had stopped among the mud and ashes to consider farther of it. A brand-new Tavern, redolent of fresh mortar and size, and fronting nothing at all, had taken for its sign The Railway Arms. And then it hoped to sell drink to the workmen. So, the "Excavators' House of Call" had sprung up from a beer-shop.'

Dombey and Son, *Charles Dickens*

The beer-shops were the priority. If the railway revolution was fuelled by steam then the labourers were fuelled by ale. The workers were the phenomenon known as navvies.

'These banditti are possessed of all the daring recklessness of the Smuggler without any of his redeeming qualities.* Their ferocious behaviour can only be equalled by the brutality of their language. They put at defiance any local constabulary force; consequently crimes of the most atrocious character are common, and robbery without any attempt at concealment has been an everyday occurrence.'

Peter Lecount, Assistant Engineer to Robert Stephenson, describing the workers on the London to Birmingham Railway (1839)

---

* What redeeming qualities did Smugglers have then?

They navigated their way across Britain so they were known as navvies. They were the rottweilers of the railway industry – they did an essential job, but no one seemed to love them. Peter Lecount said that 'every man's hand was against them' but seems shocked that 'their hand is against every man'.

Even the Romans could have advised Lecount on his obtuse inability to see he was part of the problem …

> 'When men are inhuman, take care not to feel
> towards them as they do towards other humans.'
>
> *Marcus Aurelius (AD 121–180), Roman emperor*[*]

⚙ The engineers took the glory, the investors took the profits, and the navvies took their lives in their hands.[†] They lodged in towns when they could or lived in hastily erected shacks. If the work didn't kill them, the squalor could. Most died before the age of 40.

⚙ There were many accidents caused by their drunkenness, but the contempt of the righteous public was harsh – many railway companies insisted their workers take part of their payment in beer.

⚙ And they worked on a 'piece rate' so the faster they worked the faster the beer money accumulated. That led to short-cuts and risk-taking. The consequent deaths went with the job.

⚙ It may seem at odds with the nature of the job, but they

---

[*] The last of the 'Five Good Emperors' so it may pay to listen to his wise words. Maybe Lecount and his cronies didn't read Latin.

[†] They also took other lives in their hands. Two navvies in Scotland were hanged for killing a foreman. They were hanged at the side of the railway line, *pour encourager les autres.*

were the dandies of their day. The hobnail boots you would expect. But what about the square-tailed coats made of velveteen? They were worn over double-canvas shirts and moleskin trousers. A bright handkerchief was essential, as was a white felt hat with the brim turned up. The rainbow waistcoat was their trademark and when they wanted a sealskin cap they would pay 15 shillings.

☼ In 80 years these unsung heroes built 20,000 miles of railway, mostly fuelled by two pounds of beef and a gallon of beer per day.

☼ There are not a lot of accounts from the navvies' side of the tracks because not many of them were literate. But Patrick MacGill was both literate and articulate. 'The Navvy Poet' had been brought up in Ireland and as a teen sold into farm labouring … a virtual slave. He escaped to Scotland to become a navvy. He described the life in the tenements where the workers lived …

'A four-square block of buildings with outhouses, slaty grey and ugly, scabbed on to the walls, enclosed a paved courtyard, at one corner of which stood a pump, at another a stable with a heap of manure piled high outside the door. Two grey long-bodied rats could be seen running across from the pump to the stable, a ragged tramp who had slept all night on the warm dunghill shuffled up to his feet, rubbed the sleep and the dirt from his eyes, then slunk away from the place as if conscious of having done something very wrong.'

From The Rat Pit *by Patrick MacGill (1890–1963),* * navvy poet

---

* MacGill's book, *The Rat Pit* was reviewed by the *New Statesman* alongside a Virginia Woolf novel. The reviewer said MacGill's book was

⎯ A NAVVY'S LOT WAS ⎯ NOT A HAPPY ONE

For all their cavalier lifestyle the navvy's life was usually short and violent. They created the railway revolution but were reviled for it.

> 'As to the kind of persons, they are the most uncivilized set of beings on Earth.'
>
> *Joseph Holly, census taker (1841)*

Were they really? What is the truth?

> 'I hate to advocate alcohol, violence, or insanity to anyone, but they've always worked for me.'
>
> *Hunter Stockton Thompson (1937–2005), American journalist*

Ale

Digging cuttings, laying rails, excavating tunnels and pushing wheelbarrows up embankments was thirsty work. Navvies slaked that thirst with as much ale as they could afford. If they were unfit for work the next day they'd have money deducted from their wage and be issued with meal tokens. The tokens could be exchanged for meals at the company

---

better. History has not been so kind to the Navvy Poet. Nor was the Army when he joined up. He published press articles about a soldier's-eye view of the early days of the war. The army said he was breaching security and arrested him as a spy. He was eventually released and reassigned – to Army Intelligence. (Hence the commonly held view that 'army intelligence' is an oxymoron.)

canteens and were known as 'flimsies' because of the thin paper they were printed on. But the flimsies were easily forged. Local farm labourers started dining out at the railway companies' expense. The Liverpool & Manchester Railway replaced flimsies with six-sided tokens made of brass. The navvies drank less and the farm workers went hungry again.

'I cook with wine, sometimes I even add it to the food.'

W. C. Fields

Religious crusades against intemperance were carried on by missionaries into the navvy camps. The Devil did not have all the best tunes. Many of the temperance songs were jolly ditties that stuck in the mind when a temptation to take a tot arose …

'Yes I am an English navvy, but oh not an English sot.
I have run my pick through alcohol, in bottle, glass or pot;
And with the spade of abstinence, and all the power I can,
I am spreading out a better road for every working man.'*

From 'The Quarterly Letter to Navvies' 1885

Nutrition

We think of scurvy as a disease that sailors suffered till someone discovered that citrus fruits were the answer. But on Victoria's railways scurvy was such a common complaint it became known as 'The Railway Disease'. In 1847 the Edinburgh Royal

---

* The English drunkard was clearly the target. This was a bit rich considering the lyrics were written by a Scot. One day someone will write a lament about deep-fried Mars Bars and that will be the English revenge.

Infirmary drew up a diet sheet that the company could give to workers, but they didn't take a lot of notice.

> 'Don't drink at all, don't smoke, you must exercise and eat vegetables and fruit.'
>
> *Robert Mugabe (1924—), President of Zimbabwe* *****

Accommodation

The navvy life was one of constant movement as the railway they worked on progressed. So home was usually temporary. There were some appalling conditions in shanty towns made up of damp shacks. But the majority of navvies found accommodation in nearby towns. It was a boost to the local economy as anyone could rent out a spare room in their house. As usual, greed reared its wide-jawed head and licked its lips.

> 'Every little farmer or shopkeeper who has an old outhouse, stable or cow-house, turns it into a dwelling and reaps a golden harvest by letting it to a navvy who must be housed near his work and is therefore compelled to pay a ruinous rent.'
>
> *Report by Select Committee on Railway Labourers (1846)*

At some point there must have been a baby born in a stable. That would make a great story, but who would believe it?

---

* This brutal oppressor is not generally given credit as a nutritionist. But, hey, Adolf Hitler was a vegetarian. In 2008 Mugabe's militia murdered the wife of Mugabe's political opponent by burning her alive with a petrol bomb after cutting off her hands and feet. (Report in *The Times*.) The best diet in the world doesn't preserve us from the disease called tyranny.

Appreciation

Some Victorians did wonder at the marvels wrought by the navvies. Poet Laureate William Wordsworth watched a group of navvies stop for lunch and was inspired to pen a poem of praise. But what are his words worth?

'WELL have yon Railway Labourers to THIS ground
Withdrawn for noontide rest. They sit, they walk
Among the Ruins, but no idle talk
Is heard; to grave demeanour all are bound;
Others look up, and with fixed eyes admire
That wide-spanned arch, wondering how it was raised,
To keep, so high in air, its strength and grace.'

'At Furness Abbey' by William Wordsworth (1770–1850),
English poet

'Simple-hearted men' is not the usual label the navvies were given and God was not always praised for their works.

Not that many navvies would have appreciated Wordsworth's poem. John Francis wrote *A History of the English Railway* in 1851 and said the navvies were 'unable to read and unwilling to be taught'.

He went on to give a more lurid account of the reactions to the invasion of the navvies … it resembles H. G. Wells's *War of the Worlds* …

'Rough alike in morals and in manners, collected from the wild hills of Yorkshire and Lancashire, displaying an unbending vigour and an independent bearing; impetuous, impulsive, and brute-like, regarded as the pariahs of private life, herding together like beasts of the field, owning no moral law and feeling no social tie. They were a wandering people, who spoke only of God to wonder why he had made some so rich and some so poor.[*] They were heathens in the heart of a Christian people, savages in the midst of civilization.[†] A feeling, (akin to that which awes the luxurious Roman when the Goth was at his gates),[‡] fell on the minds of the English citizens where the railway labourer pitched his tent.'

John Francis (1851)

So, let's get this right, John …. You didn't like the navvies?

---

[*] Surely, John, that's really not a bad question. In the 21st century we are still waiting to hear God's answer. 'Because I can,' she would probably say.
[†] The same 'civilization' that enjoyed nothing better than a public hanging, or rat-baiting – a blood sport which involved filling a pit with rats and then betting how long it would take for a terrier to kill them all. As for children in factories or boys up chimneys … they were the epitome of 'civilization' were they not?
[‡] A fine metaphor … except the navvies were armed with sensible shovels and practical picks, the Goths with sharp swords and dangerous daggers. And the Goths were Christians not heathens. But in the kingdom of the prejudiced the rage-blinded commentator is king.

Racism

The navvy battalions are often perceived of as Irish immigrants. In fact they were mostly English. And the Irish were often the despised and persecuted minority.

In 1846 an English foreman argued with an Irish worker about the working method as they laboured on the Lancaster and Carlisle Railway. They fought. But the story spread that the Englishman had been set upon by a mob of Irish.

> 'Rumour is a pipe
> Blown by surmises, jealousies, conjectures
> And of so easy and so plain a stop
> That the blunt monster with uncounted heads,
> The still-discordant wavering multitude,
> Can play upon it.'
>
> *William Shakespeare (1564–1616), English playwright*

The blunt monster was not stopped and the multitude of English vigilantes set out to avenge the wrong. They first destroyed the Irish camp near Penrith. An army of Irish workers marched to avenge the revenge.* The magistrates persuaded and bribed the Irish to withdraw. But the English summoned almost 2,000 compatriots to exact revenge on the avengers of the revenge.

The English workers knocked the heads off their pick-axes to make clubs … no, this was not to reduce the damage to Irish heads but to make them more manageable. Others

---

* If you wish to partake of a riot the *Westmorland Gazette* offers a practical guide, explaining the attackers were armed with 'knives, billhooks, pistols, pokers, sticks, clubs, pitchforks, hammers and other weapons'. Other weapons? What's left? Bows and arrows, perhaps?

carried spades and crowbars. They followed a red handkerchief tied to a pole – a 'bloody' symbol or, as 1889 radical
workers would sing:

> 'Then raise the scarlet standard high,
> Within its shade we'll live and die,
> Though cowards flinch and traitors sneer,
> We'll keep the red flag flying here.'*

The army was called in to halt the violence but the Irish who
were caught were badly beaten. The brawny English rebel-
leader was sentenced to transportation to Australia. His
employers said he was a 'quiet, civil, inoffensive man'.

> 'Anger is a brief madness.'
> *Horace (65–8 BC), Roman poet*

The Irish navvies near Edinburgh were entirely to blame for
beating a policeman to death while working on the Edinburgh to Hawick Railway shortly after. That was the sort
of incident that besmirched the name of the Irish navvies
forever after.

Did you know ... the great escape

In a rare show of national harmony the Welsh labourers gathered all the English and Scottish workers near
Bangor into a united band. Their aim? To drive out
all the Irish navvies. (Oh all right, not that nationally
harmonious then.) A Welsh leader was arrested as the
posse marched on the Irish camp. He was locked away
in the local prison which was besieged by his angry

* Which ironically was the official anthem of the Irish Labour Party.

friends. 'Release him!' they cried (in Welsh). But their help wasn't needed. A policeman had carelessly left a ladder in the yard of the jail. The Welsh agitator let himself out.

Like most racially motivated prejudice there is no logic to it. Racial tolerance and racial equality are seen as modern phenomena. But even in 1846 the Welsh newspaper was sighing ...

> 'Is there not enough toil, brow-sweat and heart-break without turning aside to wound a brother in the spirit of devilry, for nothing less it is.'
>
> North Wales Chronicle *(May 1846)*

The style is archaic. The message is fresh as this morning's news.

Safety

The navvies cut corners and took risks. According to the immutable laws of averages, some gamblers would lose their chips. Who was to blame for a worker's stupid actions? It wasn't until 1880 that a new law placed responsibility in the hands of the employers.

It had taken since 1846 to copy the French lead on this. They heard of a horrifying example from France. You KNOW that Fireworks Safety Code (rule 5) says, 'Never go back to a lit firework.' But an Irish navvy in France had been using gunpowder to blast rock. When a charge failed to go off ...

> 'The foolish Irishman was silly enough to go and
> blow on it. He had both his eyes blown out and both
> his arms blown off.'
>
> *William Reed, Director of Paris and Rouen Railway (1846)*

Mr Reed argued that the 'foolish Irishman' only had himself
to blame. So it was unfair that his company had to pay the
compensation. He would say that. Humanity wasn't part of
the thinking.

> 'The worst sin toward our fellow creatures is not to
> hate them, but to be indifferent to them: that's the
> essence of inhumanity.'
>
> *George Bernard Shaw*

Carelessness or indifference, drunkenness or sheer bad luck,
the accidents went on. And the blame game went on too. A
man called John Kent died at Edge Hill on the L&MR line.

> 'He was shoring up a heavy bank of clay, fourteen or
> fifteen feet high, when the mass fell upon him and
> literally crushed his bowels out of his body.' *
>
> Liverpool Mercury, *report on Edge Hill Tunnel accident*

Dangerous days.

---

* He was the first navvy to die building a railway tunnel. William
Huskisson is forever remembered as the first passenger to die when hit by
a train. John Kent is also a famous first – so why is he forgotten?

Reputation

Fear of the navvies stalked the streets. Good citizens barred their doors and closed their eyes in prayer when the navvy hordes entered their town. But the navvy reputation had its uses. At a general election a navvy mob was hired to intimidate the voters into voting for the navvy paymaster – a politician. A politician using bullying tactics on the voters? Can you believe that?

> 'I have never intimidated the masses … I only intimidate corrupt officials.'
>
> *Zhu Rongji (1928—), Chinese politician*

Some locals took advantage of the navvy reputation when the gangs of workers arrived at the Bramhope Tunnel. They began stealing sheep and were confident the navvies would be blamed. But a local police inspector was a regular Sherlock Hercule Marple and by examining footprints in the mud he was able to lay the blame at the right door.

The Irish were seen as more civilized and humane than their Yorkshire and Lancashire workmates. In 1846 the Irish famine was devastating the land and Irish crossed the sea in search of work, not trouble, and food not drink …

> 'The postman tells me that several of the poor Irish do regularly apply to him for money drafts, and send their earnings home. The English, who eat twice as much beef, consume the residue in whisky, and do not trouble the postman.'
>
> *Thomas Carlyle (1795–1881), Scottish philosopher*

Chauvinism

Some navvies took their wives along on their treks to find work. Some women were expected to do the cooking, washing, child-rearing and cleaning for all the men in their navvy hut. The idea of women's rights was barely on the horizon.

A husband was allowed to beat his wife with a stick … so long as the stick was no thicker than his thumb. There were many tales of men selling their wives for anything from 4 pence to 12 pence.*

Even if a young man was just a 'boyfriend' he treated a girl as if he owned her. One 16-year-old boy put it this way …

> 'If I seed my gal talking to another chap I'd give her such a punch on the nose it would sharp put a stop to it.'
>
> *Interview with youth*

Some men even had the nerve to say …

> 'It's an odd thing but the girls axully like a feller for walloping them. As long as the bruises hurt she'll be thinking of the bloke that gave them to her.'
>
> *Interview with man*

And even the music hall entertainers sang – with no irony – the acceptance of violence towards women.

-----

* The tale of a navvy swapping his wife for a gallon of beer is almost certainly apocryphal. A woman for beer? She'd be bitter.

> 'I must acknowledge that she has a black eye now and then,
> But she don't care a little bit, not she.
> It's a token of affection – yuss in fact that is love, ✱
> Wiv me an 'er – 'er and me.'
>
> *Music hall song, late Victorian*

But at least women didn't work as navvies in Britain. In Pisa some Italian women did help with the excavations. (Maybe Pisa women had a leaning towards it?)

Children fared no better. A young worker had his foot crushed and his navvy partner said …

> 'It's no use crying about it, lad. You'd be better to
> have it cut off above the knee.'

But children in towns like Manchester and Sheffield only had a 50 per cent chance of seeing their fifth birthday. A navvy's life was not a happy one. But it was worse in many ways for the women and children.

> 'Working in the tunnel, shovelling out the dirt,
> I worked so hard I wore out me shirt.
> The tunnel caved in and we all got badly hurt,
> Drill you terriers, drill.'
>
> *Folk song (1888)*

✱ This does not come under the definition of 'tough love'.

The statistics are grim …

> 'It was said that the workmen could lay an almost
> entire line, on sleepers, made from injured men's
> legs.'

— THE PRICE OF A RAILWAY —

Robert Stephenson's London and Birmingham Railway cost
£5.5 million but again we want to look at the cost in human
terms. His father gave him the skills he needed to build a
railway …

> 'Be careful to leave your son well instructed rather
> than rich, for the hopes of the instructed are better
> than the wealth of the ignorant.'
>
> *Epictetus (AD 55–135), Greek sage*

The L&B was a safe railway that would *transport* passengers (fairly) safely. But well-instructed Robert was not able
to *build* his railway safely. The workers were at risk every
day. Bridges were a menace because you could fall off them.
Tunnels were a hazard because they could fall on you.

When the pick-axes struck rock then the quickest solution was to use gunpowder to blast a way through. Now you
can see the problem straight away, can't you?

If the tunnel is two miles long, you have to light the fuse
then retreat a mile. The fuse would have to be absurdly long
OR you'd have to run OR you'd be caught in the blast in that
confined space.

And of course you will have seen the solution, won't you? Yes, these tunnels had vertical ventilation shafts and they were up to 200 metres long. So here is the plan …

➤ Lower a bucket down the ventilation shaft big enough to take a small team of workers

➤ Lay the charge and attach a fuse that will take (say) a minute to burn

➤ Light the fuse

➤ Retreat and climb into bucket

➤ Be hauled 200 metres to the surface, with time to spare, before the charge explodes

➤ Lower the workers and let them shovel the loose rock into the bucket

And you'll have spotted the danger in the plan? Of course you did.

The workers were known to light the fuse and retreat to the bucket and be hauled up … only for the bucket to get stuck. As the fuse fizzed the workers stood there – unable to rise to safety or go down to douse the fuse – knowing their fate. As certain and as horrifying as men standing on the gallows.

Others died before they realized the Grim Reaper was a nanosecond away. By 1876 dynamite had been invented but, wrongly handled, it was no safer than gunpowder.* In a

---

* Patented in 1867 by Alfred Nobel (1833–96) to be precise. In 1888 he was mis-reported as dead. That was upsetting because it was his brother Ludwig who had hopped the Lud-twig. The erroneous headlines screamed, 'The Merchant of Death is Dead'. He was doubly upset by the label and decided his legacy should be one of peace. Hence his last will set up the creation of prizes.

tunnel on the Llynvi and Ogmore Railway 12 men and a boy died when dynamite exploded unexpectedly.*

> 'Two of the deceased, Richard Parsons and the boy Clements, were blown to atoms; some small fragments only of their bodies having been recovered, and these fragments were found in the immediate neighbourhood of the manhole where the explosion had occurred.'
>
> *Major V. D. Majendie, accident investigation report*

The atoms of John Clements were just 13 years old. But don't worry about the poor children. The 'Gangs Act' of 1867 banned the employment of children under the age of eight.

Near Halifax two men were lowered down a shaft without realizing the bottom was flooded. They escaped with a ducking.

- ◉ Other accidents included men tumbling from the bucket if it caught an obstruction and tipped on its journey. A dark and deadly tumble would follow.

- ◉ Or you could simply stand at the bottom of the shaft and find a careless engineman had let a heavy platform drop onto your head.†

- ◉ The Bramhope Tunnel on the Leeds and Thirsk line was two miles long. In a grand Gothic gesture the owners

---

* The finger of blame points to a tunneller who was preparing the charges. A witness said he'd seen that tunneller stick a naked candle in the tunnel wall just a foot from where he was working. If oil and water are a proverbial bad mix then candle and dynamite may just be worse. The rest is history.

† Lots of ways to die in a tunnel. As the foreman may have said, 'Take your pick.'

gave the northern entrance towers and battlements. A miniature copy of the Bramhope arch was etched in Otley churchyard on the grave of the 23 men who died building it. A nice touch, eh? *****

Did you know ... shaft suffering

A series of shafts were dug along the line of a tunnel. The tunnel was dug to join the shafts – from the ends (obviously) but also from the bottom of each shaft outwards and hope the tunnels meet. (The Box Tunnel, built by Brunel on the Great Western line was one inch and a quarter out. Shocking.)

But the shafts themselves were a danger. The sides could collapse onto the workers below or they could simply be a large hole for wandering navvies to fall down at night. The official report came up with the most unlikely Bowdlerism in a quote since Caesar didn't say, 'Et tu, Brute.' The accident investigation said: *'No one saw him fall but heard a cry of Oh, dear!'*

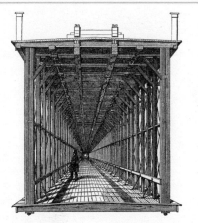

---

* Why did this not set a trend in memorials? How would you like a picture on your gravestone of the thing that killed you? A car that crushed you for a hit-and-run victim? A bomb for a Blitz victim or a large mosquito for a malaria victim?

TUNNELS AND TERROR

> 'What are all the records of history but narratives of successive villainies, of treasons and usurpations, massacres and wars?'
>
> *Dr Samuel Johnson (1709–84), English writer*

The 1830s would see Britain in a social upheaval that could have led to anarchy and agony. Riots over corn prices, fury over voting franchises that favoured the filthy rich and a new, young queen who was as popular as the plague. Victoria.**

Yet, through it all, the railways would thrive and change the face of the country for ever. Inspired engineers led the revolution. They couldn't have done it without the ardent and impassioned support of Mr and Mrs Public. The love of railways was embraced.

---

* When a lady-in-waiting, Lady Flora Hastings, developed an abdominal growth the rumour mongers said she was about to become, shock of shocks, an unmarried mother. Victoria believed the rumours and was blamed for spreading them. Lady Flora died of the massive tumour and when the young queen appeared in public she was hissed and jeered. Her popularity recovered down the years. There were to be only eight assassination attempts on her portly personage.

— ROBERT STEPHENSON —
(1803–59)

> 'Tiger father begets tiger son.'   *Chinese proverb*

Stephenson Junior. A pasty-faced youth with a weak constitution who lived in the shadow of his famous father. Many of the illustrious 'Stephenson' achievements were either joint efforts or the creation of Robert. George was offered, and took, the credit. Did Rob feel robbed?

Robert's mother died of tuberculosis when he was a toddler and his father abandoned the boy, first to a local nursemaid and then to Robert's Aunt Nellie, while he worked in Scotland. Then his fortunes (and his fortune) improved. He 'invested' in Robert. It was the most profitable investment he'd ever make.

George was …

> 'An untaught, inarticulate genius'
> *Anon, quoted by John Francis in* A History of the English Railway

George didn't have a formal education so he made sure Robert did. Robert mingled with well-off kids who didn't recognize the putative genius in their midst.

George was barely literate but pressed schoolboy Robert to share the reading of complex engineering texts from which they both learned. Evenings in the Stephenson household may not have been a riot of fun.

A wit to woo

Robert returned from his brief trip to South America when the mysterious spat with his father blew over and they launched the Liverpool and Manchester Railway.

George had stumbled and mumbled his way through the first parliamentary inquiry, confounded by the competently clever counsel. But for the re-run Robert represented their case. Quietly aggressive and capable of demolishing the barbs of the barristers.

George moved to Liverpool to supervise the building of the line. Robert was based in their Newcastle works where he constructed the locomotive that would win the Rainhill Trials.

Did you know ... *Rocket* by name

It will be known for all time as 'Stephenson's *Rocket*'. Everyone assumes that means George Stephenson built it and it stands as a monument to his genius.

But it was Robert Stephenson who built it. Stephenson's *Rocket* all right, just the wrong man gets the vulture's share of the credit, as usual.

While George focused on the L&MR and Rainhill preparations, Robert went on to win the Whitstable and Canterbury contract in 1828. Anyone with a modicum of geographical knowledge will exclaim, 'That's a long way from Tyneside. Why Whitstable?'

In a word ... love. In three words, love of Fanny. For before he went to America Robert had fallen for fair Fanny

Sanderson and now he wanted a London-based project to facilitate the wooing.*

They married in 1829, four months before the Stephenson family triumph at Rainhill.

The eager engineer

Robert was accumulating commissions like a schoolchild accumulates nits. He was learning the hazards and the horrors by trial and error. Or, in the case of the Leicester coalfield line in 1831, trial and terror.

The Glenfield Tunnel hit a bed of sand and the delays doubled the cost. Then the contractor, Daniel Jowett, fell down one of the working shafts and died. That occasioned further delays. (How inconsiderate of Jowett.) At the same time it was a little hint of tunnel tribulations to come.

Another job was a Warrington and Newton line linking the Liverpool and Manchester Railway to a proposed line to London. The fly in the ointment was that Rob was committed to a particular route and the L&MR under George Stephenson were opposed to it.

'Family quarrels are bitter things. They don't go by any rules. They're not like aches or wounds; they're more like splits in the skin that won't heal because there's not enough material.'

F. Scott Fitzgerald (1896–1940), American author

---

* The W&CR was the first railway to be run primarily for passengers. It beat the L&MR. It got top-of-the-range engineer Rob Stephenson. Why? Because it was prestigious and important? No. Because of a stray arrow from cupid. You could call it an arrow-gauge railway perhaps … or perhaps not.

George Stephenson won the battle then screwed it up by falling out with his star engineer, Joseph Locke. In a bizarre arrangement, Geordie and Joseph were each given half of the line to build. Geordie's young (but cheap) assistants put in such incompetent estimates George even managed to lose his half of the contract.***** Locke took over.

Rob Stephenson must have had a chuckle about that.

The greater loss for George was the end of his partnership with the efficient Joseph Locke. Locke teamed up with a rising young contractor, Thomas Brassey, and together they would go on to become the greatest railway-building team ever.

But when the next big contract came along Robert remembered his father's careless neglect of details. The company George Stephenson and Son was given the contract for the *survey*. But there was no 'George Stephenson and Son' on the contract for the *building* – Stephenson Junior was in sole charge. What sort of family debate went on there? The quiet boy was rising above the blustering father.

Father and son had already fallen out over the improved locomotive designs Robert was building. Robert built *Planet* with cylinders inside the wheels and created the most powerful loco around in 1830. George grumbled that it broke more crankshafts. *Planet*'s design succeeded.

Having outshone his dad in the building of locos, the young man was now taking over the building of lines too.

> 'The meek shall inherit the Earth, but not its mineral rights.'
>
> J. Paul Getty (1892–1976), Anglo-American industrialist

---

* A viaduct at Penkridge was estimated by the cheapest contractor at £26,000. Geordie's serfs had guesstimated it would cost £6,000 and had only allowed that much. The passengers would be miffed if they reached Penkridge and had to wade across the River Penk because the bridge ended a quarter of the way across.

— THE BIRMINGHAM BEHEMOTH —

Forget pioneering Stockton and Darlington, forget glitzy Liverpool and Manchester, forget little Whitstable and Canterbury. This was a massive task. It was the building of 112 miles of the London and Birmingham line.

It was an awesome task for a man not yet 30. It was an awesome task for any man. Robert had secret doubts – wouldn't you? But a report from his fellow engineers was a stirring encouragement.

'Let nothing deter you from executing the work in the most substantial manner so it may serve as a model for all future railways and become the wonder and admiration of posterity. Let me conclude with the advice of Queen Elizabeth to one of her courtiers: *Climb boldly then.*'

J. U. Rastrick, report to London and Birmingham
Railway Company (1833)

This wonder to all posterity would bring prestige to Robert Stephenson. It would bring death to many navvies.

The Watford Tunnel disaster

'The histories of mankind that we possess are histories only of the higher class.'

Thomas Malthus (1766–1834), British cleric and economist

Each tunnel seemed to create its own problem. The ones under the River Thames were built into clay that was so fluid it was like tunnelling into quicksand. A tunnel should have been lined with an overarching wall of bricks. For the London and Birmingham line, in the tunnel at Primrose Hill, the mud squeezed the cement from between the new-laid bricks then ground them to dust. George Stephenson said ...

'London clay would rather run uphill than stand still.'

He had to use extra-hard bricks and quick-setting 'Roman' cement.

When Robert Stephenson came to the Watford Tunnel he must have expected an easy ride through the chalk. But the navvies discovered the chalk held pockets of gravel. When they broke through, the gravel rained down on their heads like bullets ... and hard hats hadn't been invented.

A typically tragic accident occurred on a July morning in 1835.

☼ Thomas Jordan, a widower, was a mine overseer so he was skilled at excavating tunnels. He was part of the early shift on the Watford Tunnel. He probably rose around 5 a.m., said goodbye to two children and set off for work. Just another day.

☼ Jordan and ten other men were lowered into one of the shafts of the Watford Tunnel. They reached the bottom of the shaft where the tunnel had been dug about three metres to either side. The roof was held up by wooden supports. Bricklayers would come in and build a permanent lining. As safe as houses.

☼ Jordan had been lowered on a platform held by a rope wrapped around a drum ... known to the workers as a 'gin'. The ride was bumpy and it hit the bottom with a knee-jarring thud. Jordan's task was to remove the temporary wooden supports. The chalk roof would hold up long enough till the bricklayers arrived on the day shift … wouldn't it?

☼ The winch operator heard a cry of 'Beware!' As he watched he saw the top of the shaft crumble and debris fall into the shaft. The hole in the ground became a gaping chasm.

☼ The operator jumped away from the abyss, became tangled in the machinery and survived. The dog that had been lying by his side tumbled down and died. Such is the tiny margin between life and death.

☼ The winding machine followed and crashed down onto the tunnellers who had just been lowered.

☼ Robert Stephenson hurried to the scene and was there within an hour. As a team of 60 tried to unearth the victims they heard groans from beneath the rubble … 36 hours after the roof-fall. Stephenson was in time to see 'portions of the remains of four men' sticking out of the rubble.

☼ An inquiry said that when the men removed the wooden frame it triggered a fault in the limestone that allowed it to collapse onto them. Safe as glass houses. A report to the company directors said that, 'the event will not have the effect of delaying the completion of the tunnel.' Oh, let's be thankful for large mercies then.

As with any disaster, the ghoulish were soon on the scene …

'In the course of a few hours thousands were drawn
to the spot, and the scene that occurred is
indescribable. The wives and families of those who
were employed about the works might be seen
running to and fro in a state of frantic despair,
ignorant which of them had been bereaved of their
husbands.'✱

Buckinghamshire Herald, *August 1835*

Our intrepid reporter made it his business (in the public
interest) to be present when the corpses were finally reached.
His account leaves nothing to the reader's imagination …

'It is presumed the poor fellow was looking upwards
at the moment he met his death, have heard the cry
of "beware" from the men at the top of the arch; his
face was crushed and the legs broken.'

Think of Victorian ladies and you think of their tight corsets
obliging then to sniff at the smelling salts at the first hint of
nature red in tooth and claw. They must have been falling
like conkers in a gale when they read the *Herald* report on
the identification of the bodies.

✱ The reporter clearly viewed the ghouls with distaste. Yet he made the
curious observation that the morning shift would have killed far more
men and 'have been awful in the extreme'. Yet, for the women and children
who lost husbands and fathers, it couldn't have been more 'awful'.

> 'Several of their relatives were in the shaft when the
> men were dug out (in which they assisted), but they
> were scarcely able to recognize a feature, as
> decomposition had taken place to such an extent as
> to render positive and perfect recognition almost
> impossible, the dress of the deceased men forming
> the only clue to identity.'

Cost of timber to shore up the tomb while the bodies were recovered: £1,000.

Amount collected on behalf of widows and relatives: £300.

The inquest had to apportion blame. The jury charged the contractors a token £5 fine because, 'every possible care and attention that skill and science could dictate had been used on the part of the company in the construction of the shafts'.

Thomas Jordan and his labourers were hastily buried and, almost as hastily, their sacrifice was forgotten.

The Stephensons had marble busts to their name. Victims like Huskisson did too ... *his* marble statue shows him clad in a toga like a Roman emperor.

The navvies who died in the Watford Tunnel Disaster? Nothing.

> 'Man toils, and strives, and wastes his little life to claim—
> At last the transient glory of a splendid name,
> And have, perchance, in marble mockery a bust,
> Poised on a pedestal, above his sleeping dust.'
>
> *From* Fame *by Andrew Downing (1815–52), American writer*

The busts all went to the ones who made the money.

DANGEROUS DAYS DEATHS IV

ROCK FALL

Victim: Thomas Jordan

Taphophobia, the fear of being buried alive, is said to be the most common fear we have, and not just amongst tunnel workers.

The tunnel collapses above you, all lights are quickly extinguished. Under the inevitable force of gravity many tons of soil, rock and gravel fall towards you. Everything goes pitch black just as you are hit by the falling debris. Thrown to the ground by the impact you are powerless to do anything.

Dirt fills your mouth, screaming is impossible. Rapidly your body uses up its last oxygen, your brain feels like it's on fire, every part of you wants to breathe but you can't. Most probably the falling rocks will have added a few broken bones to the experience, but before the pain can register you will lose consciousness. Your brain dies about four–six minutes later with no oxygen, but then trapped under tons of earth you are not going anywhere.

Dr Peter Fox

The real tragedy

The loss of life was all the more tragic because the Watford Tunnel was unnecessary. It was only built to appease local landowners who were worried the railway would spoil the view from their land if it ran over-ground.

Ten men died so a landowner could look out on green fields.

Fifteen years later one of the navvies explained the neglect of the men who moved mountains …

> 'There wasn't no chance to save a halfpenny – and now half of us walk about and starve, or beg, or go to the workhouse.'
>
> *Henry Mayhew (1849)*

The Kilsby killer

In 1838 the Kilsby Tunnel on the L&BR was to be a mile and a half long. 'Passengers will suffocate,' the gloom-mongers said.

'There is too much quicksand – a canal tunnel had to be abandoned,' the doom-mongers predicted. Rob Stephenson was suspected by the money-men of being too young and inexperienced to cope with the massive problems.

The contractor, James Nowell, died exhausted by the Kilsby effort. Further down the line contractor Hughes ended up paralysed and contractor Chapman's heart would fail.

> 'That which does not kill us makes us stronger.'
>
> *Friedrich Nietzsche*

Horse-feathers. Mr Nietzsche may have been a very clever man, but he was born ten years too late to work on the Birmingham Railway or he may have revised that opinion. What doesn't kill us leaves us half killed.

> 'Robert Stephenson infused into the workmen so much of his own energy that when either of their companions were killed by their side, they merely threw the body out of sight and forgot his death through their own exertions.'
>
> *John Francis (1851)*

Robert Stephenson didn't grow stronger. He took to smoking cigars (like rival Brunel) and sought comfort in Victorian drugs.* It took its toll on his fragile body. His chain-smoking of cigars didn't help his delicate constitution. He probably suffered depression and one biographer, Jeaffreson, guessed he would welcome death.

Was he able to enjoy his success through the stress? Did the navvies have a poorer but a better life?

> 'A crust eaten in peace is better than a banquet partaken in anxiety.'
>
> *Aesop (620–564 BC), Greek storyteller*

In 1838, four painful years after it was started, trains ran from London to Birmingham. Robert Stephenson's triumph was

---

* An observer said the stress of the L&BR 'would lead him to very frequent recourse to the fatal aid of calomel'. Those who took this mercury chloride compound to excess found that their teeth and hair fell out. Robert's didn't, so he was not an extreme addict, but it must have shortened his life. It was usually combined with opium. Robert reported that it was prescribed by his doctor.

soured by the company directors, whose report suggested the huge overspend was the engineer's fault. 'A stain on my character,' he complained.

> 'Verily I say unto you, No prophet is accepted in his own country.'
>
> *Luke 4:24*

The Tanfield Trauma

> 'I'm up to me eyes in debt. I wisht I was taller. A man come to our door. I says come in, take a seat. He says "I'm coming in to take the lot."'
>
> *Bobby Thompson (1911–88), North-East England comedian*

Robert Stephenson's Birmingham success was short-lived. In 1839 he was a director of a weird and wonderful mineral line from the Stanhope quarries to the ships on the Tyne. Instead of taking cash he took £500 worth of shares. It was a huge error of judgement.

Greedy landowners demanded extortionate compensation for granting permission to cross their land. And when the company began to run up debts, Robert realized it wasn't a 'limited company'. The shareholders were liable for the debts … even if their shares were freebies in lieu of cash.

As poisoned chalices go, Robert's £500 share certificate was neat cyanide and arsenic with a bouquet of mustard gas. The debtors came to him with demands for £50,000. He was perceived as the richest director so they knocked on his door first. His earnings as engineer to the London and Birmingham Railway was £2,000 p.a. Oooops!

A lesson for us there. *Always* look a gift horse in the mouth. Or don't look at one at all.

> 'Marry me and I'll never look at another horse!'
>
> *Groucho Marx*

With the help of new investors he reduced his debt to £20,000. It was more than he had in the bank so he was reduced to selling a half-share in Robert Stephenson & Company to his father. That must have hurt.

Another way of raising money was for Robert to complete the railway from Darlington to Newcastle. This was part of a dream scheme of the Pease family. They were the loyal backers of the Stephensons on the Darlington and Stockton Railway. But they weren't paying the sort of money young Robert needed to fill the hole in his bank balance.

The reprobate George Hudson, on the other hand, was ready to splash the cash … Not *his* cash, of course. All Robert had to do was persuade Joseph Pease to invest in a different scheme (Darlington south to York) then take George Hudson as a partner on the Newcastle venture.

Robert was selling the virtuous Pease family's dream to an unscrupulous rival. Back-stabbing is too kind a term for his treachery. The Pease consortium were livid. Director Captain Watts described the Newcastle line and its backers as …

> 'An abortion with a crooked back and a crooked snout, conceived in cupidity and begotten in fraud.'

Did the money justify the means? Would you sell friendship for a pot of gold? Can you be both rich and righteous as the Pease family were?

'Is it possible to succeed without any act of betrayal?'

Jean Renoir (1894–1979), French film director

The thirties ended on a low note then.* Never mind, there was worse to come.

BRIEF TIMELINE – THE FORTIES

1840   The first excursion train run for trippers. The starting point is Sheffield. The exotic holiday location? Derby.†

1842   Women and children under ten are banned from mines. John Bean (a 'piteous youth') tries to shoot unpopular monarch Victoria. A report by Edwin Chadwick on sanitation brands Glasgow as having the filthiest slums in Britain.

1843   Men dress as women in the 'Rebecca Riots' in Wales. They protest against road tolls. The expanding railways will sort that problem.

1844   The new 'Railway Act' says all trains must make provision for third-class passengers.‡ Charges no more than one penny a mile, minimum speed 12 mph and all carriages covered. The railways stretch from London to Tyneside now and George

---

* He said he could have borne it if it had been bad luck. But his distress was brought about by 'men who are indebted to me'. Rather like Caesar's assassination without the cutting edge. Et tu, brutes.

† Thus proving the old adage, there is no accounting for taste.

‡ In 2014 the concept of third class was revised. A bitter commuter complained that in his experience it had never gone away.

Stephenson is praised at the opening as the man who built the first-ever locomotive.*

1845   The Irish Famine sends thousands in search of work on the railways. Desperate Irish prepared to work in appalling conditions to make a crust … or a crisp.

1846   Select Committee on Railway Labourers says the navvies are 'hard worked and often exposed to great risk of life and limb'. Understatement. Why couldn't the Committee save words and say 'they died in their hundreds'? Famine spreads to Scotland where (weird but true) relief is in the hands of Sir Edward Pine Coffin.

1847   A lucky girl has her arm amputated at Richmond hospital. 'Lucky' because she is the first beneficiary of 'anaesthetic'.

1848   10,000 miles of track now. Meanwhile in Europe it is the Year of Revolution – a series of political upheavals – but within a year, the revolutions have collapsed like the Watford Tunnel. George Stephenson's life reaches the terminus.

1849   George Hudson, railway entrepreneur and rogue is ruined. Now he knows what it's like for his victims.

---

* A blatant distortion of the truth. Yet George Stephenson, who was present at the banquet didn't care to disabuse the sycophants. Richard Trevithick's spirit should have turned up as the ghost at the feast.

EPIDEMICS AND ERRORS

THE MADNESS OF
THE MONEY-MEN

> 'The history of all countries and all ages is but a sort of mask, richly coloured. The interior working of the machinery must be foul.'
>
> *John Quincy Adams (1767–1848), US President, diary 1822*

The 1840s were a terrible time to live. If the diseases didn't kill you then the factory machines in the workplace and the railways would. And if you survived then, for most, it was eating foul food in the impoverished, insanitary slums that drove you to terrible toilets … while dodging cruel criminals on the way.

Oliver Twist, in the Charles Dickens novel of 1838, shone a light on the 'interior working' of the workhouse culture and the crime-infested 'rookeries' of the cities. Life had always been bleak for the underclasses. But the 1840s saw the middle classes sleep-walk towards ruination as they were hypnotized by the lure of the locomotive world.

> 'Annual income twenty pounds, annual expenditure
> nineteen pounds, nineteen shillings and six pence,
> result happiness. Annual income twenty pounds,
> annual expenditure twenty pounds nought and six
> pence, result misery.'
>
> *Mr Micawber in* David Copperfield *by Charles Dickens*

The 1840s are known as the era of 'Railway Mania'. New railway companies were hatching like eggs from the Golden Goose and salivating speculators scrambled, scurried and scuttled to secure their share of the shining shells. But eggs break. Even through their greed-twisted visions of wealth, the speculators knew that. But they always thought they'd get out before the crash and the losses would happen to someone else.*

The poor wanted to be rich. The already-rich wanted to enjoy their wealth in comfort.

> 'Why, gentlemen, if this sort of thing be permitted
> to go on you will, in a very few years, *destroy the
> nobility.*' †
>
> *Sir Astley Cooper (1769–1841) to Robert Stephenson*

---

* Emily and Anne Brontë had shares in the York and North Midland Railway Company. In 1845 sister Charlotte advised them to sell the shares before the bubble burst. They ignored her advice and lost their money. Clever big sister Charlotte … to her the dreams of railway riches were just castles in the Eyre.

† Sadly the railway failed to do what the guillotine did much more efficiently in France.

The aristocracy could defend their land with legal delays and demands for compensation. The poor didn't have that luxury. A line from Greenwich, to the east of London, was carried in the sky across to London Bridge. A vast viaduct of 878 arches and four miles of rails was built over the worst slums London could boast. Bill Sikes would have felt at home there – and his real-life, career-criminal counterparts certainly did.

If your slum had to be demolished to make way for a pillar of the viaduct then you were promised that a cottage would be built for you under the arches. It would be worth the upheaval, the money-men smiled. (One may smile, and smile, and be a villain, as Hamlet discovered.) Your cute cottage was never built.

And the upheaval was more than just having to move from your home. Your miserable life was made worse by the warring navvies using your mean streets as battlefields – two gangs working on different sections: the English Ground and the Irish Ground. They were supposed to be allies on a great venture, not rivals. They didn't see it that way. Best not to be in the way when the rival mobs met.

Yet a cracked skull was preferable to an invisible enemy that arrived in 1848: the deadly disease cholera. It spread its tentacles through the shabby and sordid streets, adding to the sorrows of the slum-dwellers. Even the warring navvy nightmare was preferable to the killer cholera that carried you off.✱

✱ Not that you'd be safe from the railway's depredations even if you were dead. If your grave was in the way of the line then you would be moved … or sometimes just your headstone. In Leeds these headstones were laid (reverently I'm sure) on the embankment where they remain to this day. The trains pass over the corpses. A true skeleton service.

⌐ BLUE DEATH ⌐

'The blanched cheeks of the people that now came out
to stare at us, were white as vegetables grown in the
dark, and as we stopped to look down the alley, our
informant told us that the place teemed with
children. Fevers prevailed in these courts we were
told more than at the side of the ditch.'

*Henry Mayhew, 'A Visit to the Cholera Districts of Bermondsey',
the* Morning Chronicle: *Labour and the Poor, 1849–50*

John Harnold arrived by the steamer from Hamburg where
the cholera was rife. He left the ship, and went to live in
Horsleydown, London. He fell ill with cholera and died in a
few hours.

How did he die?

DANGEROUS DAYS DEATH V

CHOLERA

Victim: John Harnold

Cholera is caused by a bacteria called Vibrio Cholerae.
It's a devilish little germ that infects your small bowel
and if left untreated kills most of the people who catch it.

It gets into you via drinking water that has other
people's faeces in it, or by eating food washed in con-
taminated water. Not nice, but it is added flavour to an
otherwise bland drink. Five days later the most watery
and profuse diarrhoea imaginable pours out of your
bottom, coupled with copious vomiting.

Typically a person with cholera loses around 10–20 litres of fluid per day, rapidly dehydrating to a crisp, while spreading the bacteria far and wide. Due to this rapid fluid loss your kidneys pack up, the salts in your blood drop and the amount of blood circulating falls. This gives you a nice blue-grey dehydration tinge to your skin, but then you die.

Of course we know now that electrolyte replacement fluids, coupled with the occasional use of antibiotics, will help people survive cholera. Good sanitation and hygiene practices have also prevented its spread.

Dr Peter Fox

Harnold's leaving gift was the bacteria that killed him. You can't blame the Cholerae. After all they had to find new, fresh bodies to exist on ... and meanwhile they lived happily in the cess pools and water pipes of the poor.

Snow right

The first major British outbreak of cholera in 1831–2 brought terror to the city of London. People simply fled, if they could afford to ...

'The first of January 1832 is mournfully distinguished as the day in which one of the morning papers announced "The Scourge" is present in Southwark; who will ever forget the panic that followed; London was comparatively deserted within 24 hours. Six hundred cases were bulletined as having occurred along the Borough bank of the Thames – in those crowded lanes where so many Irish people herd, pent up as in a leper-hospital.'

Thomas Hawkins (1810–89), English fossil collector: Memoirs (1834)

The clues are there – the fact the crowded slums are the breeding ground of the disease. But in those pre-Victorian days no one made the connection and understood the way that disease spread. A few people noticed that the 'night soil' men, who emptied the toilet waste, seemed to live long and healthy lives. One of the people to make the connection was Dr John Snow.

During the 1848–9 outbreak, Snow set out to show that cholera was usually carried in the water supply.

Snow roamed the streets, testing water and interviewing families about their drinking habits. John Snow's examination of a water sample from a public water pump in Broad Street suggested a London outbreak arose from people drinking from it. He famously disabled the well pump by removing its handle. Modest Dr Snow said he didn't save THAT many as the epidemic was already in rapid decline.

A public health survey confirmed that bad habits in the mean streets were a gift to the disease …

'As we gazed in horror we saw a little child lower a tin can with a rope to fill a large bucket that stood beside her. The inhabitants put the mucky liquid to stand, so that they may, after it has rested for a day or two, skim the fluid from the solid particles of filth, pollution, and disease. In this wretched place we were taken to a house where an infant lay dead of the cholera. We asked if they really did drink the water. The answer was, "They were obliged to drink the ditch, unless they could beg a pailful or thieve a pailful of water."'

Henry Mayhew, 'A Visit to the Cholera Districts of Bermondsey'

— THE DEAD-END LINE —

The cholera outbreak of 1848–9 caused a new headache for London: what to do with the dead.

The London Necropolis Railway was a railway line opened in November 1854 by the London Necropolis Company (LNC) to carry corpses and crying mourners between London and the newly opened Brookwood Cemetery 23 miles south-west of the city.

A railway service for coffined corpses. In a crowded metropolis like London it solved the problem of over-flowing graveyards. Some of those graveyards were already looking to move the skeletal remains elsewhere to make room for … guess what? Yes, new railway lines.*

It wouldn't do to have coffins in carriages. The Bishop of London argued that it would be highly inappropriate to convey the coffins of working-class people in the same carriage as respectable folk. Or, worse, let your corpse share a carriage with the remains of your moral inferiors. The dead good couldn't mingle with the dead bad …

> 'It may sometimes happen that persons of opposite characters might be carried in the same conveyance. For instance, the body of some profligate spendthrift might be placed in a conveyance with the body of some respectable member of the church, which would shock the feelings of his friends.'
>
> *Bishop Charles Blomfield (1852)*

---

* The shifting of corpses from a Manchester cemetery left a terrible stench. When in 1865 it came to skeleton-shifting at St Pancras in London the railway builders were much more careful. The local authority sent along a young man to inspect the grisly work. He was Thomas Hardy, the soon-to-be-famous author. He made sure the corpses were reburied discreetly – far from the madding crowd, I guess.

A dedicated station was built, adjacent to Waterloo. It had its own stations along the way so the public would not be alarmed at sharing a ghost train. Locals named them 'The Dead Meat Trains'.

Naturally some superior stiffs (and loved ones) had to be carried in a first-class compartment. Even in death there is snobbery. Church of England ex-worshippers were not expected to share a carriage with Nonconformists.* They had separate cemetery areas at Brookwood too, each with its own station. First-class ticket-holders got a private service – third-class were allowed a communal one.

Did you know … third-class death

The Great Western Railway staff were instructed not to offer assistance to third-class passengers. When John Jonathan was found frozen half to death in a third-class carriage the staff broke their rule and carried him out of the carriage when it arrived at Bath. However it would never do to have a passenger die on GWR property so they deposited him on the pavement outside the station … where he died.

There are even shocking stories that a second-class passenger was left outside to die. What did the poor man pay the extra for? He should at least have been refunded the difference.

---

* It makes you wonder what happened when they got to Heaven. Separate clouds? Afterlife apartheid? Saintly segregation? The gravestone of two navvies may hold a clue. It reads: 'The line to Heaven by Christ was made / With heavenly truth the rails are laid' and concludes: 'Come then, poor sinners, now's the time / At any station on the line / If you'll repent and turn from sin / The train will stop and take you in.'

For the mourners, refreshments were served in the restaurant and there was time for a stroll around the graves before the train took you back to the London of the living.

It was all very un-Christian. One person who attended a funeral at Brookwood was Mahatma Gandhi. As he said …

'I like your Christ, I do not like your Christians.
Your Christians are so unlike your Christ.'
Mahatma Gandhi (1869–1948), Indian nationalist leader

At the time Brookwood Cemetery was the largest cemetery in the world. It was planned to offer a good home to all the deaths in London for centuries to come. They'd sell a lot of one-way tickets of course … or of corpse.

The LNC was looking to corner the bountiful body trade. After all …

'In this world nothing can be said to be certain,
except death and taxes.'
Benjamin Franklin (1705–90), US Founding Father

People keep dying despite the efforts of doctors – and sometimes because of the efforts of doctors.

The cemetery was far enough from London to stay unaffected by urban growth, but of course it relied on the new railway to make it viable. No one wanted to follow a horse-drawn hearse for 23 miles. Yet it was never the success the LNC hoped. Rival companies diverted your dear departed to nearer graveyards and funeral trains dwindled to one a week. You could say the LNC had stiff competition. The terminus was terminated by a bomb in the Blitz of 1941.

Today only the London façade of the terminus near Waterloo is still there. At the Brookwood end the tracks and the stations are gone and only the station chapels remain as a remnant of a late, lamented line.

— SWEETER SLUMS —

> 'Poverty is the worst form of violence.'
>
> *Mahatma Gandhi*

The railway companies claimed they were performing a social service and improving public health by demolishing slums – they wiped out the district of Agar Town north of St Pancras, a blight of back streets and pestilence. But Somers Town to the north of the slums was a more pleasant residential district. Those houses were devoured by the iron monster too. There was little thought given to rehoming the displaced underclasses.

Profits came first and the hypocritical railway companies would have shrugged and smiled, 'That's the price of progress.' They weren't THAT committed to social service. In 1874, when most of the damage was done, a law said the railway companies were responsible for re-housing the evacuated. The companies shrugged and smiled again … and largely ignored the law.

Around 120,000 people were forced to move to make way for the Victorian railways.

— DEATHS IN THE FAMILY —

The forties were a bad decade for Robert Stephenson. In 1840 his beloved wife Fanny was diagnosed with an incurable cancer. She died two years later.

'My dear Fanny died this morning at five o'clock.
God grant that I may close my life as she has done.
Her last moments were perfect calmness.'

Robert Stephenson, diary entry 4 October 1842

Fanny begged him to remarry so a new wife could give him children she had not. He never did. He moved house and no sooner moved in than a fire destroyed his new home and all his possessions. Robert never seemed to get the breaks.

'Luck is my middle name. Mind you, my first name is Bad.'

Rincewind in Interesting Times, *Terry Pratchett*

After two years of cancer, with primitive Victorian pain relief, Fanny's death must have been 'a kindness'.

Three years later George Stephenson's wife Elizabeth reached the end of the railroad. He married his housekeeper in 1848 but didn't survive for long.[*] In August 1848 George suffered a fresh attack of pleurisy.

Robert was completing a new triumph, a bridge at Conwy in North Wales. When his father fell ill he was sent for and arrived at George's house in Derbyshire on 12 August 1848, just in time to be at his father's side as the old man died. George had seemed indestructible but died at the age of 67.

He was mourned as a national treasure. A friend said, 'He should be lying in Westminster Abbey, not a country churchyard.'[†]

---

[*] George didn't consult Robert about his third marriage and it came as an unpleasant shock to his son. Robert was not amused. Father and son fell out – for the last time.

[†] George and Robert had turned down knighthoods on several occasions. Would a Westminster Abbey burial have suited the cantankerous man?

One man quietly confided to his diary that Geordie's death, like Fanny's, was a blessing … but for a very different reason. Edward Pease had been the driving force (founder and funder) of the Stockton and Darlington Railway 30 years before. Now, at the age of 80, he witnessed the demise of George Stephenson with mixed feelings. At the funeral, he said …

> 'I had a serious, friendly conference with Robert and expressed to him that it was a kindness his father had been taken, his habits were approaching to inebriety. I fear he died an unbeliever.'
>
> *Edward Pease, diary entry 17 August 1848*

George Stephenson, atheist and drunk. Not the sort of obituary that the Victorian press would print. The *Derby and Chesterfield Reporter* was respectful … while being a teeny bit ambiguous …

> 'What faults he had, (and who will pretend that he was without them), cease to be remembered now that he is no more. We shall not look upon his like again. Nay, we *cannot*, for in his sphere of invention and discovery there cannot again be a *beginning*.'

It's a shame no one wrote those last two sentences for Richard Trevithick.

As George Stephenson was lowered into his grave, 'Railway King' George Hudson was being heckled by angry shareholders of the failing Eastern Counties Railway.*

By coincidence the great age of Railway Mania was dying at the same time as George Stephenson.

---

* The only quiet moment in the stormy shareholders' meeting was when Hudson asked for a minute's silence to remember his friend Stephenson. It was a calm in the middle of a storm. A storm that signalled the wreck of the Hudson empire.

BRIEF TIMELINE —THE FIFTIES

1851   'The Great Exhibition' at Crystal Palace showcases
        Britain's ingenuity. The six million visitors arrive
        mostly by rail, organized by Mr Thomas Cook's
        company. The tracks now extend to 7,000 miles
        under 200 competing railway companies.

1852   The Duke of Wellington goes to the great boot
        locker in the sky. Special trains are laid on from
        as far away as Aberdeen so people can go to his
        funeral. Britain's first public flushing lavatory opens
        in Fleet Street.

1853   Australia refuses to take any more convicts. Prince
        Albert develops holiday home for Queen Vic,
        Balmoral Castle in Scotland, now more accessible
        because of the railways. Smallpox vaccination
        made compulsory. The Woodhead Tunnel through
        the Pennines opens after costing many navvy lives.

1854   Britain is at war with Russia in the Crimea. A
        mighty crew of navvies will travel to build railways
        for the war effort. The hard-drinking (tight
        brigade) can't save the charging Light Brigade.

1855   Great Gold Robbery from a train between London
        Bridge and Folkestone in England.

1857   Victoria's empire shaken by massacre of 200 Brits at
        Cawnpore in the Indian Mutiny.

1858   Charles Darwin publishes *The Origin of Species*.*
        A new public drinking fountain near London's
        Old Bailey offers an alternative to cholera- and
        typhoid-infested street pumps.

---

* Warning: this Darwin bloke is trying to make monkeys of us all. Let
your mirror be your guide.

1859   Robert Stephenson and Isambard Brunel die. The Geordie genius (aged just 55) gets a spectacular state funeral. Queen Vic allows the cortège to pass through Hyde Park where 3,000 tickets are sold to spectators.*

― BRILLIANT BRUNEL ―

'Though an able and ingenious man, Brunel himself has no experience in railways and seems to hold in slight regard the judgement of those who have.'

Railway Times *(1838)*

Isambard Kingdom Brunel (1806–59) was another bright flame of Victorian genius who was snuffed out before he could retire with the honour he deserved. He died at 53, even younger than Robert Stephenson, who hopped the twig within weeks at the age of 55. Dickens was 59 … and, like Brunel, saw his father thrown into debtor's prison. The two also shared Portsmouth as their birthplace.

Brunel was a man who thought outside the box. George Stephenson went for railway lines 4 foot 8 inches apart, Brunel designed the Great Western Railway with lines 7 foot apart.

Of course there were objectors to a line heading west from London. But one was a little unusual. The Provost of Eton College wittered that the coming of the railway would allow …

---

* Did you know (amaze your friends with this trivia) Robert Stephenson was godfather to the founder of the boy scouts. The man who made fire by rubbing two boy scouts together was christened Robert Stephenson Smyth Baden-Powell. Not a lot of people know that. You do now.

'… the most abandoned of London's inhabitants to come down by the railway and pollute the minds of the scholars.'

Brunel triumphed – but only at the cost of a substantial bribe to Eton and the cost to the minds of the Eton boys who have no doubt been polluted ever since.*****

In a 2002 poll Brunel came second in the list of 100 Greatest Britons (runner-up to Winston Churchill).**†** George Stephenson doesn't make the top 10 (65th) and Robert doesn't even make the list. Brunel's talent was not so warmly appreciated in his lifetime. He was reckless with investors' money and some of his ideas were brilliantly impractical …

'We do not take him for either a rogue or a fool but an enthusiast, blinded by the light of his own genius, an engineering knight-errant, always on the lookout for magic caves to be penetrated and enchanted rivers to be crossed; never so happy as when engaged "regardless of cost"**‡** in conquering some (to ordinary mortals) impossibility.'

Railway Times *1845*

---

* Parliament, that old Etonian boys' club, said there was to be no station in Slough, near the school, so the boys couldn't hop on a train and pollute their minds in the slums, stews and fleshpots of London. The railway company bought a pub and used it as a station. The incensed Provost took them to court … and lost.

† There were mutterings that students at Brunel University campaigned hard and distorted the Greatest Britons' poll result. Of course the list was pretty wacky anyway with Guy Fawkes (30), Johnny Rotten (87) and David Beckham (33) being included. True greats like you and me are missing. Pfffft!

‡ Brunel didn't live to see his SS *Great Eastern* sail on her maiden voyage. It was well over budget (though the contractor may have been largely to blame). When it finally made its first voyage in 1860 it proved too uneconomic to be commercially viable – 35 paying passengers and a crew of 400, quite apart from the coal-guzzling boilers. The light of the knight's genius blinded him to the realities of making money.

The rebel railway to the west was safer and smoother than the 'narrow' gauge … but doomed to fail when the rest of the country adopted Stephenson's measurement.*

So this Great Briton polymath was a bit of a loser. And, like so many of his compatriots, he suffered his share of dangerous days. Not just on railway projects either …

☼ **Tunnels** In 1828 he was working in the Thames tunnel for his engineer father. The sewage that leaked in, along with noxious gases, was a health hazard. But not so hazardous as when it flooded. Two senior miners died and Brunel was seriously injured. The tunnel was abandoned for seven years. Loser.

☼ **Bridges** In 1831 Brunel won a competition to design the Clifton Suspension Bridge in Bristol. But he didn't get to build it. The Bristol riots stopped work and commercial confidence was so damaged the building was cancelled soon after it was started.† It was completed by Brunel's colleagues in 1864 as a tribute to him after he died. Loser.

☼ **Transcontinental railway** George Stephenson's ambition was to run railways from London to Edinburgh. Brunel wasn't so lacking in ambition – he made plans

---

* An 1846 law insisted all British main lines should be the Stephenson gauge. Brunel was beaten.
† The riots were as dangerous as the railways. When a troop of dragoons charged a mob of rioters 4 rioters were killed and 86 injured. Some rebels probably died in the fires they themselves had lit. In 1832 a hundred of the mob were brought to trial; four were hanged. Brunel had been sworn in as a special constable so we know he was on the side of the law … but that didn't get his bridge built. Relatively gentle times of course; the anti-Catholic 'Gordon Riots', just 50 years before, had seen 285 people shot dead, with another 200 wounded and over 30 hanged.

to run them from London to New York. His Great Western trains would steam to Bristol where passengers would board the SS *Great Western* and SS *Great Britain*. The venture failed when his company lost the valuable transatlantic mail contract to Cunard. Loser.

☼ **Inventions** Not satisfied with steam power, Brunel devised the atmospheric railway. The train is pulled on a piston in an air-tight tube between the rails, through a sealable slot. In 1847 it was trialled on the Exeter to Teignmouth stretch of the South Devon Railway. The pipes corroded and leather seals rotted. A story went around that the leather had to be lubricated with animal fat. The regional rats loved this dripping sandwich and chewed it to destruction. It seems this was just a mischievous myth put around by mockers. George Stephenson dismissed the atmospheric idea as 'humbug from beginning to end'. Robert reserved judgement till he saw it tried and found wanting. Failure.

☼ **Steamships** Of course Brunel was famous for building the world's first screw-driven, iron-hulled steamships. But one prize eluded him – the glory of being the first steamship to cross the Atlantic. In 1838 the little paddle-steamer *Sirius* was in competition. Brunel sneered that *Sirius* was too small to carry the fuel needed to cross the Atlantic. His SS *Great Western*, the largest ship in the world, would win. But as he was due to set off a fire broke out below decks and, when Brunel went to inspect the damage, he fell down the steps and seriously hurt himself. SS *Great Western*'s start was delayed by four days but charged off in pursuit. SS *Sirius* ran out of fuel just short of New York as Brunel predicted. But the captain started burning the ship's furniture and even a mast to steam to the end and win by a day. Brunel lost. Again.*

☼ **Architecture** In 1851 the Great Exhibition was planned to showcase Britain to the world. Almost 250 designs were rejected. Brunel put forward a long, brick exhibition hall with a cast-iron dome and it looked likely to get the green light. But a last-minute entry from Joseph Paxton (dubbed the Crystal Palace) defeated the Brunel design. It was a little cruel of Brunel's pal Robert Stephenson to declare that Paxton's palace was 'A thousand times better than anything that has been brought before us'. Below the belt, Rob.

☼ **British Railway** Apart from the ill-fated Great Western line Brunel came head-to-head with the Stephensons in Northumberland in 1844. Landowner Lord Howick was blocking George Stephenson's plan for a railway through the Borders that would complete the link from London to Edinburgh. Howick turned to Isambard Brunel for a rival scheme. The words 'red rag' and 'bull' spring to mind. For Stephenson Sr and Brunel had the mutual antipathy of bull-fighter and bovine.

---

* The story of an Atlantic ship crew burning the ship to finish the journey may sound familiar. The writer Jules Verne used that true tale as part of his famous adventure story, *Around the World in Eighty Days*. *Sirius* crossed back and never sailed the Atlantic again. Nine years after her great Atlantic adventure she was caught in a storm off the coast of Ireland and sank. Twenty people were drowned. The SS *Great Western* trip took a record 15 days and over the next eight years made 60 crossings. But it wasn't 'the first'.

'Stephenson was too much given to look upon railways and engines as belonging to himself alone and that no one else had the right to meddle with them. Forgetting that he himself was the follower of Trevithick and others. He never forgave Brunel for taking the wide gauge.'

Civil Engineer and Architect's Journal *(1848)*

The added grief was that this was a railway through the heartland of Stephenson territory. And on top of that Brunel was proposing to use the (untried) atmospheric railway system, not the locomotive-driven standard the Stephensons had set. In the end it was George Hudson's wealth and influence that defeated Brunel who retired with his tail between his legs. Defeated.

Brunel's SS *Great Eastern* was the death of him. He collapsed on the deck of the ship with a stroke and died a fortnight later. But at least he left a memory of the man and his work, which is more than many have in history.

'Vain the ambition of kings who seek by trophies and
     dead things
To leave a living name behind, and weave but nets to
     catch the wind.'

John Webster (1580–1634), English Jacobean dramatist

— WOODHEAD WOE —

A Woodhead Tunnel looked so problematic that in 1830 the great George Stephenson abandoned his survey. This three-mile monster had to be hacked and hewn and blasted and battered through Pennine rock. In 1835 the job went to Charles Vignoles, who had worked under Stephenson on the Edge Hill Tunnel on the L&MR. He didn't get on with the Great Curmudgeon. Vignoles' version of their animosity was as acid as old vinegar …

> 'I plead guilty to having neglected Mr S's favour by crying down all other engineers, especially those in London. For though I highly respect his great natural talents, I could not shut my eyes to certain deficiencies.'
>
> *Charles Vignoles (1793–1875), railway engineer*

The deficient Mr Stephenson said that problems on the Edge Hill project were Vignoles' fault and took pleasure in sacking him.

Then Vignoles was handed the survey contract for the Sheffield, Ashton-under-Lyne and Manchester Railway. Sneering Stephenson said it was so far beyond Vignoles' capabilities he would eat the first train that came through the tunnel.

The tunnel DID open in 1845, but Charles Vignoles had fallen out with the railway company.* He resigned in 1839

---

* Yes, he was a great one for falling out, but that was par for the course, it seems, with these early engineers. In this case the directors were at fault. They were penny-pinching, squeezing, wrenching, grasping, scraping, clutching, covetous, old sinners. When forced to provide accommodation for the navvies they refused to send huts for the Pennine winter. They sent tents instead.

before work started. So the world was deprived of the pleasure of seeing Geordie eat an engine.*

The tunnel contractor excavating from the western end was the ruthless Wellington Purdon.† Some of his working methods were murderous. Take the example of the unfortunate William Jackson …

➤ Miner John Webb drilled a hole in the rock of Woodhead Tunnel and packed it with gunpowder.

➤ Webb packed the gunpowder into the hole with an iron rod as William Jackson looked over Webb's shoulder.

➤ The iron rod sparked on the rock, ignited the gunpowder and propelled the rod out like a rocket-propelled spear.

➤ It went clear through Jackson's head, killing him instantly.

➤ When an inquiry asked Wellington Purdon why he hadn't used a safe and spark-free copper ramrod he said copper was too soft to do the job. (The truth? Copper was too expensive.)

➤ Asked why he didn't use the new safety fuses that burned reliably and predictably, Purdon claimed they were a slower way of working and time was money. He made the barely credible statement: 'I would not recommend the loss of time for the sake of the extra lives it would save.' So another man died for the sake of a few pennies.

'Capital is reckless of the health or length of life of the labourer, unless under compulsion from society.'

Karl Marx (1818–83), German revolutionary socialist

---

* He could have eaten a locomotive with salad. Rocket is very tasty.
† He started out as a labourer on the S&DR and even by the standards of the day was a slave-driver.

Marx said that a capitalist must always be forced to care for the safety of the workers. Purdon's answer to the committee of inquiry who dared suggest such a thing?

> 'I have a great aversion to anything like government officers interfering with details in the case of engineers.'

There you have it. In the railway age the 'engineers' were gods – not to be challenged or rule-bound, confronted or contradicted. The workers were simply 'details'.*

The contractor for the eastern end of the tunnel was the kind-hearted Thomas Nicholson. If his workers died then tender Tom promised he would guarantee, 'A good oak coffin, provided at my expense.'

What more could any of us ask?

If there was any worth in the Woodhead woe it was that the scandal gave publicity and shone a light on the dismal navvy life. Marx's 'compulsion from society' came into play. Nothing would ever be quite so bad as the Woodhead workings again.

Did you know ... Hackworth's pride

Timothy Hackworth's last loco design was *Sans Pareil II*. He built it in 1849 and was so confident in its power his son, John, challenged George Stephenson's son, Robert, to a race from York to Berwick. It seems Stephenson declined.

---

* A banquet was held to celebrate the opening of the line. The directors thanked Mr Purdon. 'His work did him the greatest credit.' (Applause.) Mr Purdon graciously acknowledged their compliments and said, 'The work had been a stiff job.' (Applause and laughter.) The un-thanked navvies rested un-remembered in their un-marked graves.

And if you're ever asked in a pub quiz who built the first locomotive to run on a Russian railway the answer is NOT Ivan the Terrible … It was Timothy the Terrific Hackworth.

'The ideal of a railway is one that comes about a mile from one's own house and passes through a neighbour's land.'

The Earl of Powys (1860)

Woodhead's woeful story was not over. In 1847 a second tunnel was started alongside the first. It was easier. Fewer men died … until 1849. A plague was sweeping through Britain and when it reached Woodhead 28 workers, in their unsanitary shanties and shacks, perished as painfully as their predecessors had in rock falls and explosions.

The men had returned from a Whit weekend break, weakened from spending their pay on ale instead of food. As they dropped like clay pigeons, the company thoughtfully sent a supply of new coffins to the tunnel site. Six hundred of the seven hundred workforce fled.

The name of the plague was 'cholera'.* Weakness of 'character' was blamed for, of course, such weakness led to drunkenness. When sober 25-year-old James Green died it was a shock to the medical experts.

---

* Dr Harrison of Manchester had experience of this disease in the 1832 outbreak and applied the same cure – liberal doses of port wine. It failed, so he switched his medicine to brandy and coffee. That failed too. How disappointing. But it should not discourage us from drinking brandy and coffee in the hope of avoiding cholera.

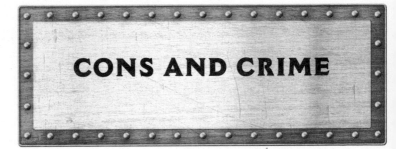

CONS AND CRIME

'History is nothing but a tableau of crimes and misfortunes.'

Voltaire (1694–1778), French writer, historian and philosopher

The railways were new. It took very little time for the sinister side of the human mind to work out ways to make an illicit profit from the national obsession.

'All railways are public frauds and private robberies.'

Colonel Charles Sibthorp, MP for Lincoln (1844)

People with money saw the railway profits and were like sharks in a feeding frenzy. And the people who didn't have money borrowed it in the expectation of making vast profits.

We know the path to wealth is never that simple. We think of the Victorian age as one of Christian rectitude, righteousness and integrity. But when it came to the railways the good Christians ignored the Bible's advice to 'lay up for yourselves treasures in heaven, where neither moth nor rust doth corrupt, and where thieves do not break through nor steal'.

Nor were they very fussy about whom they sank their shark teeth into. The wealth was an illusion, a bubble that the shark teeth would one day burst.*

The Liverpool and Manchester Railway was proving a great success. Interest rates were falling, so the planned new lines looked like a great way to make a fast buck. More money poured into new schemes and the price of shares rose.

In 1846 alone almost 10,000 miles of new lines were approved in 272 acts of Parliament. Only two-thirds would ever be built. Some were over-ambitious. But others were just plain fraudulent.

> 'There's a sucker born every minute.'
>
> *P. T. Barnum OR David Hannum (American showmen)*
> *OR half a dozen others (1869)* †

Charles Ponzi made a fortune in the 1920s with his scheme to sucker investors.‡ A Ponzi scheme pays dividends to its investors from their own money or the money paid by later investors, rather than from genuine profits. Others see the amazing dividends and throw money at the charlatan. When the fund is cash-rich the fraudster vanishes, trousering the remaining money.

---

* And if you don't mind we'll drop the shark metaphor now. You have the general idea: uncontrolled ruthless greed.

† P.T. Barnum is credited with the saying, but it seems he didn't originate it. It was an argument over a carved-stone giant which rival David Hannum claimed was a petrified man. Barnum offered $50,000 for the fake. When Hannum refused, Barnum had his own copy carved. Hannum made the 'sucker' comment about the crowds who paid to see Barnum's creation, even though it had been exposed as a fraud.

‡ Ponzi started out his life of crime by writing out a cheque in a cheque-book he found lying around in a company's offices. He forged the director's signature. Simple. He was caught. His investment cons eventually failed and after a spell in prison he died in poverty. So did many of the investors he'd relieved of their life savings.

Mr Ponzi (who was caught) did not invent the scam. Charles Dickens was describing such schemes 80 years earlier in *Martin Chuzzlewit* and *Little Dorrit*.

> 'Credit is a system whereby a person who can't pay, gets another person who can't pay, to guarantee that he can pay.'
>
> Little Dorrit, *Charles Dickens*

The great Charles Ponzi of the Victorian railway era was George Hudson MP. An interesting character who ended up being the victim of a 'virtual' beheading in York.

The story of Hudson's rise and fall could have been the plot of a Dickens novel.

GEORGE HUDSON (1800–71) AND HIS GRAVY TRAINS

> 'Never give a sucker an even break.'   *W. C. Fields*

George Hudson made things happen. He wasn't an engineer, he was a wheeler and dealer. As a railway historian wittily said …

> 'He became rich by keeping everything but his accounts.'
>
> *Adrian Vaughan*, Railwaymen, Politics and Money *(1999)*

Hudson was a farmer's son and his tale was one of riches to more riches to rags. He inherited £30,000 and used it to buy power.*

He began by becoming Mayor of York. His lavish banquets – at the rate-payers' expense, of course – earned him lots of brownie points with the men of power and the fat cats. Then, by chance, he met George Stephenson in Whitby and learned of the engineer's dream of a rail line from London to Newcastle. It would bypass York, so Hudson decided to remedy that and build a link to put his city on the railway map. The meeting could have derailed the meteoric Stephenson career …

> 'Unfortunately George Stephenson was introduced to George Hudson; still more unfortunately, Faust was not inattentive to Mephistopheles.'
>
> *Joseph Devey,* The Life of Joseph Locke *(1862)*

George Hudson began his reign over trains by driving through the construction of the York and North Midland Railway. It was such a success his future investors and partners would be dazzled into gold-blindness like moles in the midday sun. Maybe he had fiddled the accounts right from the start and those profits were all an illusion. The public believed in him as a man who could do no wrong.

> 'Time, which alone makes the reputation of men, ends by making their defects respectable.'
>
> *Voltaire*

* Hudson's uncle was dying. The solicitous young George spent time at his bedside. His reward was the £30k inheritance. That's the way to do it. Mind you, Hudson later whined, 'It was the worst thing that had ever happened to me.' He was like the lottery winners whose fortune ruined them.

○ How did he become the 'Railway King'? He fashioned new railways (with other people's money) and amalgamated with existing lines (bought cheaply) so he created monopolies. He then became MP for Sunderland and used his influence to pass bills in Parliament that would favour his railway companies. At one time he was said to be canvassing support for 16 of his projects. By 1844 Hudson had control of over a thousand miles of railway.

○ Hudson then began to pay large dividends from new capital investment … which attracted more new capital investment. Classical Ponzi but, in Victoria's Britain, not a crime. And, of course, a fair share of that loot went in the Hudson suit pockets. He continued to pay unreal dividends and more companies wanted him on their boards. He accepted … so long as they made him chairman, accountable to no one. When directors of the railway companies dared to question his accountancy he threatened to resign.* That shut them up.

> 'It is not power that corrupts but fear. Fear of losing power corrupts those who wield it, and fear of the scourge of power corrupts those who are subject to it.'
>
> *Aung San Suu Kyi (1945—), Burmese opposition politician*

○ Hudson was thriving in a free-market economy. (If it got any freer it would have dropped off.) But the essence of free market is 'competition'.

---

* At least that was the tale they told when Parliament finally got around to investigating the fraud. When Hudson demanded money, like Baa-baa Black Sheep, they simply said, 'Yes, sir, yes, sir, three bags full.'

> 'Whether we fall by ambition, blood, or lust,
> Like diamonds we are cut with our own dust.'
>
> Duchess of Malfi, *John Webster (1580–1634),*
> *English Jacobean dramatist*

Hudson's nemesis was competition in the shape of the Great Northern Railway. In 1846 this shorter and more direct link between London and the North was put to Parliament. Hudson used all his influence to try to block it. The legal fees for the battles were an enormous: 12 per cent of the capital costs of building it.

> 'Doctors are the same as lawyers; the only
> difference is that lawyers merely rob you,
> whereas doctors rob you and kill you too.'
>
> *Anton Chekhov (1860–1904),*
> *Russian playwright and author*

And that capital was a formidable £5.6 million.

This was at the height of the Railway Mania.* Where would the labour come from? And the investors' purses must have been empty? And the Railway King was throwing his considerable influence against the Great Northern. It couldn't succeed.

It did.

The Great Northern – with its direct line to Newcastle and beyond – was good news for some of Hudson's companies – the York and North Midland for one. Bad news for others – the Midland. He resigned from the

---

* Between 1845 and 1847 there were proposals for 7,500 miles of railways with a grand budget total of £138 million. You don't get much more manic than that.

Midland but the halo had slipped and the glow was starting to shine on those shadows that he wanted hidden.

Did you know ... morbid mania

There was a feverish flurry of applications in 1845. Rivals in the Railway Mania raced to Parliament to stake their claim to a new project before the deadline. One company desperately needed to travel on the railway of a hostile rival. They dressed in black and acted as mute mourners while they hid their plans in a coffin. The rival even laid on a special train for the artful adversaries. Dead crafty.

When the house of cards collapsed it took down not only Hudson but the Railway Mania.

An inquiry found he had stolen shares and 'diverted' £600,000 from his own companies. Parliament set up an investigation and discovered – shock/horror – he had bribed MPs.[*] He was briefly imprisoned for debt in York Castle in 1866.[†] He fled to Paris and lived there in poverty.

Oddly, one of the men who predicted a financial collapse was George Stephenson. He advised his solicitors ...

---

[*] Of course Parliament is made up of those same MPs. American cowboy Will Rogers probably had it right when he said, 'A fool and his money are soon elected.'

[†] Appropriately the prison that hosted Dick Turpin before his execution. Turpin was a thug and a sadist, who robbed and tortured and killed, but is remembered as a 'gentleman of the road'. Hudson was a visionary who reshaped the history of Britain and is remembered as a crook. Strange world.

> 'I hope you have kept clear of the mania of wild railway schemes – thousands of people will be ruined as I have learned that many have mortgaged their little properties to get money; of course their properties will be lost up to the amount they have got.'

He was also becoming disillusioned with George Hudson …

> 'I have made Hudson a rich man, but he will very soon care for nobody unless he can get money from them.'

Wise after the event perhaps. Stephenson avoided the Mania and clung on to his wealth. Hudson didn't. He stayed as MP for Sunderland until 1859 but was ruined.

Hudson was detested by Dickens …

> 'I feel disposed to throw up my head and howl whenever I hear Mr Hudson mentioned. If you can let me know anything bad of him, pray do. Something intensely mean and odious would be preferred, but anything bad will be thankfully received.'
>
> *Charles Dickens*

But the greatest ignominy was reserved by the council of York City … the very place he had made the centre of the railway world. Hudson was famous for his vow to 'mek all t'railways cum t'York' and he pretty well succeeded.

Was the city grateful? No. His statue was not erected in a place of civic pride. Instead Hudson's marble head was removed and replaced by that of a new favourite. Cruelly it was that of George Leeman, Hudson's rival and arch-enemy. Even George Hudson Street was renamed Railway Street.

Maybe they should have left it there as a lesson to us all in vaulting ambition, like Ozymandias in Shelley's fantasy …

'And on the pedestal these words appear –
"My name is Ozymandias, king of kings:
Look on my works, ye Mighty, and despair!"'

'Ozymandias', Percy Bysshe Shelley (1792–1822), English poet

Maybe have as an inscription Hudson's philosophy …

'It's morally wrong to allow a sucker to keep his money.'

W. C. Fields

The real Victorian villains

George Hudson is the bête noire of Railway Mania. The greedy and the foolish who had flocked to give him their money turned against him as his schemes unravelled …

'Most people rejoice at the degradation of a bloated, vulgar, insolent, purse-proud, greedy, drunken blackguard. An upstart, who had nothing to recommend him but his ill-gotten wealth.'

Charles Greville, Clerk to the Privy Council, Diary 1849

The crooked criminal that destroyed lives through monstrous greed. But in truth he had a legion of willing helpers. They were a class of people known as politicians.

'Peers and members of the Lower House were avowedly engaged as traffickers in the railway market.* Members attached to "the railway interest" voted for each other's projects. There was in those years scarcely a person who was not personally anxious that a bill should be obtained for some new line.'

J. C. Jeaffreson, The Life of Robert Stephenson (1866)

It's been said that only one man has ever entered Parliament with honest intentions. Like Hudson, that man was from York. His name was Guy Fawkes.

When the overpriced shares were rendered worthless there was real agony and destitution. It seemed every town saw its share of suicides. Those seedy and devious Members of Parliament were happy to let Hudson take the blame.

Hudson's greater sin was to drive down costs at the expense of the safety of his employees and their passengers. His North Midland Railway was reputed to be more dangerous than any in Britain. Rival companies took to putting up spoof posters at stations offering to let NMR passengers book a burial plot at the same time as they booked their ticket.

When he cut train crews' wages they resigned en masse. He replaced them with cheap, barely competent, scabs. Within days a goods train on the NMR line smashed into a passenger train at Barnsley with fatal results.

Yet some appreciated the good he did for the Industrial Revolution …

---

* The Lords too? Oh, God, he is including the bishops and archbishops then. Heaven help us … as the bishops helped themselves.

'Hudson was a man of great discernment, possessing a great deal of courage and rich enterprise. A very bold, and not at all unwise, projector.'

William Ewart Gladstone (1809–98),
Liberal politician, MP and Prime Minister

Courageous or crooked? Or just an enigma?

— ROBERT'S END —

As the forties rolled on through the age of Railway Mania the Stephensons generally prospered. George Hudson had said of the Stephensons …

'I am only a tool in the hands of genius.'

The truth was the Stephensons had been tools in the hands of Hudson.

Great engineers like Brunel and Locke concentrated on the grand designs. Robert Stephenson had to worry about the locomotive works in Newcastle as well.

When George Stephenson died in 1848 Robert bore the full weight of the Stephenson brand. He'd lost his wife and father, he had come close to ruin with the Stanhope Railway investment. By 1850, at the age of 47, the emotional and physical strains had exhausted him and he did no more great work of note for the remaining years of his life.

At least he was reconciled with the Pease family. Edward died, aged 91, in July of 1858.

Robert became close friends with Isambard Brunel too, in spite of the latter's rivalry with Geordie Stephenson.

When Brunel collapsed after the trial run of his SS *Great Eastern* he didn't know his rival and friend Robert Stephenson had taken to his bed with his final illness. Robert died four weeks after Isambard at the age of 55. The death certificate recorded 'congestion of the liver', but it was the deadly doses of mercury that hastened his end.

Robert was accorded a state funeral.* Engineer Joseph Locke helped bear Robert's coffin. Within six months Locke too had died. In 1859 the Grim Reaper must have been planning a railway.

> 'Robert Stephenson, Brunel and Locke died before
> their time. Their triumph was also their tragedy.
> With their deaths a great era of heroic endeavour
> drew to a close. For good or ill they laid the
> foundations of the modern world.'
>
> L. T. C. Rolt, George and Robert Stephenson (published 1960)

The greatest tribute to Robert had come from Isambard Brunel. IKB (for once) did not compare Robert to dad George … he compared Robert to himself …

> 'He is decidedly the only man in the profession whom
> I feel disposed to meet as my equal or superior.'

You cannot imagine George Stephenson ever admitting to that sentiment, can you?

---

* Robert's biographer, Jeaffreson, had a theory that the public had had ten years to realize the mighty George had been slighted by the small-town burial. Robert's state funeral was a tribute to them BOTH. Poor Robert. Even in death he was haunted by the shade of his father.

— CRIME TIMES —

> 'Now, for your shame, a Power, the Thirst of Gold,
> That rules o'er Britain like a baneful star,
> Wills that your peace, your beauty, shall be sold,
> And clear way made for her triumphal car.'
>
> *William Wordsworth*

Wordsworth may have admired the achievements of the navvies but he didn't like the impact of the railways on the landscape. A bit of consistency would be nice, Mr Poet Laureate.

> 'Hell is a city much like London –
> A populous and smoky city;
> All are damned – they breathe an air
> Thick, infected, joy-dispelling.'
>
> *Percy Bysshe Shelley*＊

That's more like it, Mr Shelley. London was becoming a smoky Hell. And Hell, by definition almost, is full of criminals. And the railways attracted undesirables of many sorts.

＊ You'll see Shelley died before the railway age got going, yet managed to create a prophetic image of industrial London. He was never appreciated in his lifetime, and never became poet laureate … which may be why his poetry was 7.35 times as good as Willy Wordsworth's.

— CRIME ON THE TRACKS —

The 'Great Gold Robbery' of 1855

'For a short time we lived quietly. But this could not last. White men had found gold in the mountains around the land of winding water.'

Chief Joseph (1840–1904), leader of Nez Perce tribe

The love of money is the root of all evil.* Railways became so reliable they could be safely used to carry quantities of gold. It was only a matter of time before a bullion train was robbed.

The 'Great Train Robbery' of 1963 is legendary. But its ancestor was the 'Great Gold Robbery' of 1855. On the night of 15 May three locked boxes of gold were sent from London to Folkestone and on the railway boat to France. When the boxes landed at Boulogne they were weighed and one box was found 18 kg light. The other two were OVER weight. Despite this oddity the boxes were sent on to Paris.

When they were opened it was found that lead shot had been substituted for the gold. The big clue was the weight discrepancy at Boulogne – the switch had happened before it reached France.

Four plodding police forces arrested hundreds of suspects … but charged no one. The British police claimed that it was a fiendish French felony. The French gendarmes that it was a

---

* To be accurate this Biblical phrase in Latin is 'Radix malorum est cupiditas' meaning 'The root of evil is greed'. We have to get this right or there will be a pedants' revolt.

cunning Kentish crime. It was a true mystery and beyond the wit of four police forces to solve. It was an impossible crime.

> 'The impossible could not have happened, therefore the impossible must be possible in spite of appearances.'
>
> Murder on the Orient Express, *Agatha Christie (1890–1976),*
> *English mystery writer*

Over a year later a career criminal and gold robber, Edward Agar, was arrested for a cheque fraud and sent to a prison hulk on the Thames. When he discovered an associate had failed to pass a lump of the loot from the 1855 robbery to his girlfriend he decided to squeal and snitch, spill the beans, blab, babble and betray.

Agar said a former railway employee, William Pierce, had had duplicate keys made. He explained that with the help of the guard they had swapped the lead for the gold before the train had reached Folkestone.

Pierce was sentenced to two years in prison – even though he had masterminded the scam; his crafty lawyer found a loophole in the charges. The guard was sentenced to 14 years transportation to Australia.* His was the greater crime … betraying the trust of the public. If you can't rely on a guard then on whom can you rely?

Pierce had promised to care for Agar's partner. If he'd kept that promise then the crime could be unsolved to this day. For the want of a few shillings a week. But the greedy man betrayed Agar so Agar betrayed them all.

---

* In the 1979 film version of the story the gentleman thief is played by Sean Connery, so of course he escapes and lives happily ever after. With a bound Agar was free? Or with a Bond he was free. If only life were like the movies.

> 'I believe, Messieurs, in loyalty – to one's friends and one's family and one's caste.'
>
> Murder on the Orient Express, *Agatha Christie*

Agar died in an Australian penal colony many years later. Before he died, a broken man, a newly arrived prisoner told him that he had become a legend in England's underworld.

Agar said, 'That means nothing, nothing at all.' An accurate epitaph.

Pierce too was succinct in his recollection. He simply said, 'I wanted the money.'

Pocket pickers and vicars

> 'I am not a timid man, but I never enter an English railway carriage without having in my pocket a loaded revolver. How am I to know but that I may have as fellow companion in the isolated lock-up I occupy a madman escaped from confinement or a runaway criminal? And what protection have I against their assault if it should please them to attack me, but in the weapon I carry?'
>
> *Letter to* The Times *1854* ✱

Travelling by train, despite the occasional disaster, was generally safe. The bigger danger to the innocent passenger was extortion and robbery.

Trains were home to card sharps, thimble-riggers (con-men who played the shell game), pickpockets and muggers.

✱ The writer was American. Say no more.

How could you select a 'safe' compartment? Get into that one with a vicar at the window, perhaps? No. The gentleman in a dog collar was probably a con-man in disguise. At one time it seemed that the Church of England had done a wholesale swap with the prison service.

Shady ladies

> '*Three* wise men – are you serious?'   *Anon*

So avoid the cleric in the corner. Try that compartment with a single lady? No. You could well be the victim of blackmail.

Imagine your surprise when she turns to you and says gently, 'I'm going to open the window at the next station and scream for help. I'll tell the transport police you attacked me. You'll be arrested and locked away. It'll be in all the papers. Would you like that?'

When you protest, 'But I never touched you!' she will smilingly reply, 'Your word against mine, old chap. Of course if you pay me a fiver I may keep quiet about your disgusting improper advances upon my person.'

'The improper advances I never made?'

'They're the ones. A fiver please.'

'That's blackmail.'

'An ugly word. Ugly … but accurate. Pay up.'

Menacing gents

'A gentleman is simply a patient wolf.'

Lana Turner (1921–95), American actress

Of course the problem for women travellers, alone in a compartment, was that they could be joined by a predatory male.

In 1875 Colonel Valentine Baker was found guilty of an indecent assault upon a young woman called Dickensen. (No victim anonymity in 1875 then.) He'd entered her compartment and chatted pleasantly. The conversation turned more personal and included the timeless chat-up line, 'You must kiss me, darling.' She declined ... wouldn't you? Then the colonel attempted to embrace Miss Dickensen and reached under her skirts.

She did not reply with the Victorian melodrama staple cry, 'Unhand me, sir!' Instead she simply screamed. No one came. She pulled the communication cord. It didn't work.

The distraught lady opened the door of the carriage and climbed out onto the running board. There she stayed till she reached the safety of the next station where the driver and guard stopped since they had seen her predicament.

Colonel Baker said he had done nothing, but the sharp-eyed guard reported that only one of the man's trouser buttons had been fastened – a bit of a clue to his intentions, perhaps?

The officer (but not a gentleman) was a pillar of the community, married, an eminent cavalry soldier and friend of the Prince of Wales. He was cashiered from the army and fined £500 and sentenced to a year in prison. A gentle-lady wrote to her daughter ...

> 'What is to happen if officers behave as none of the
> lowest would have dared to do unless a severe example
> is made? Colonel Baker has a very bad moral character.'
>
> *Queen Victoria, letter to daughter Louisa*

The case aroused great public interest, but it was not a rare occurrence, nor was it the first.

In 1851 a man had made lewd suggestions to a 'respectable female' as they travelled from Preston to Lancaster. He tried to kiss her and her clothes were torn in his struggles to get inside them. Complain to the police? Don't bother; he *was* the police – Superintendent Henshall of the Westmorland Constabulary. He was later dismissed from the force for irregularities in his expenses' claims. But the assault on the lady occasioned just a £5 fine.

An accused man would usually try to turn the tables on his victim and discredit her.

> 'At Lambeth police court on Friday, a lady obtained
> a summons against the incumbent of a large and
> influential parish in the metropolis and also a
> popular preacher for indecent behaviour towards
> her in a railway carriage.
>
> 'The charge was dismissed, in consequence of some
> levity in the woman's habits, and the clergyman, we
> believe, stands acquitted in the opinion of the religious
> society in which he was very highly esteemed.'
>
> *1859 Newspaper reports*

'Twas ever thus.

Assaults on women continued and invariably the victim fled from the carriage. In one spectacular case the lady climbed onto the carriage roof.

The battered hat 1864

The advice was to travel with a friend, for your own protection …

'In going through a tunnel it is always as well to have the hands and arms disposed for defence so that in the event of an attack the assailant may be immediately beaten back or restrained.'

The Railway Traveller's Handy Book *(1862)*

One man who hadn't read the book, or who found the 'arms disposed for defence' tactic failed to help, was Mr Thomas Briggs.

'I'm very proud of my gold pocket watch. My grandfather, on his deathbed, sold me this watch.'

Woody Allen (1935—), American writer and actor

Thomas Briggs, a banker, was the victim of the first murder on a British train. The 69-year-old clerk was beaten to death and thrown onto the line while heading for Hackney on the 21.50 from Broad Street to Poplar in July 1864.

The motive was clearly robbery as his gold watch and chain, and gold-rimmed glasses, were found to be missing.

A passenger entered the compartment to find gore on the floor. Soon afterwards old Thomas Briggs was spotted near the tracks by an engine driver. Briggs was seriously injured. He was carried to a nearby pub* for treatment

---

* The pub he was taken to was the Mitford – later renamed the Top o' the Morning – in Cadogan Terrace, Bow. It's been modernized except for the back room where the bludgeoned banker Briggs was treated. You can see the table where he lay … if that's the sort of thing that rows your boat.

then taken home, where he died the next morning from his injuries.

It caused a public panic. The press were happy to pour petrol on the flames of train terror ...

'As news of the murder spread a feverish fear emerged. It was said that no-one knew when they opened a carriage door that they might not find blood on the cushion, that not a parent would entrust his daughter to the train without a horrid anxiety. That not a traveller took his seat without feeling how he runs his chance.'

Daily Telegraph

Questions had already been asked about what a person could do if they were taken ill or needed assistance in these carriages with no corridors. What nobody anticipated was for a first-class passenger, travelling on a short journey home, to be murdered.*

There was an empty bag, a walking stick and a crushed hat – a hat that did not belong to Mr Briggs.† A thug on the train had beaten the old victim and stolen his watch. Or, in the underworld slang of the time ... a blodger on the Mary Blaine gave a dewskitch to the dillo pidgeon and half-inched his jerry.

Police Inspector Tanner of the Yard finally found clues and witnesses that pointed to a German immigrant called Franz Muller. Muller had left on a ship to New York. The police

---

* Mind you second- and third-class passengers weren't expecting to be murdered either. But, somehow, the outrage of Mr Briggs being in first class was more ... outrageous.

† A tip here for wannabe murderers. If you are going to murder someone for their hat do NOT leave your own hat behind to identify you.

DANGEROUS DAYS DEATH VI

BLUNT WEAPON TRAUMA

Victim: Thomas Briggs

The heavy stick hits your head at speed, compressing the skin against the underlying bone. Instantaneously the skin splits right down to the skull, arteries and veins tear, causing blood to splatter through the air as the bones shatter. The force of the blow quickly accelerates your head and brain in the opposite direction of the impact only to be stopped by your neck. Your head suddenly decelerates, closely followed by the delicate brain hitting the inside of the skull. Like a jelly dropped onto the floor it mushes and splits, your lights go out, you are unconscious and so miss the splitting headache of the experience and any further blows.

Where you are hit broken fragments of bone are pushed into the brain tissue, causing more damage, while torn blood vessels bleed into the space around the brain. In the enclosed space of your skull, with nowhere else to go the blood builds up, the pressure squashing and pulping your brain further. As brain cells die the vital messages sent to the heart and lungs telling them to work stop. Not breathing and with no heartbeat, you die.

Dr Peter Fox

inspector left on a faster ship, arrived first and arrested the German, who was taken back to trial. He was found guilty and hanged in front of an appreciative audience in November 1864.

Muller had Thomas Briggs's hat and watch, while his own distinctive hat was the one left behind in the carriage. Open-and-shut case really, in spite of 21st-century efforts to cast doubt on his guilt. (The conspiracy theorists conveniently forget Muller confessed to the hangman.) The alternative theory is that banker Briggs had rejected a loan application and was repaid (with interest) by a crack or two to the skull.

It was Muller whodunnit.*

Brighton bludgeoning

> 'You haven't even bothered to get the complete evidence … And there was a third man there. I suppose that doesn't sound peculiar to you?'
>
> *Dialogue from* The Third Man *movie (1949)*
> *by Graham Greene (1904–91), English writer*

In 1881 Frederick Gold died in an assault that had echoes of Thomas Briggs's murder. He was stabbed, shot and thrown from the carriage window on the train from London to Brighton.

The chief suspect was a young man, Percy Mapleton, found covered in blood when he staggered from the empty train carriage. Percy claimed there had been three of them in the carriage; the killer (the third man), had shot at him, stunned him and left him for dead. The same man must have

---

* Those in denial please send your objections on the back of a £20 note to the author.

accounted for Frederick Gold. But Percy's head wound was more like a knife cut than a bullet graze.

He was released after questioning but accompanied back to his London home by a detective. As the detective waited for Percy to change out of his blood-stained clothes, the young man slipped out of the back door and fled. Oooops.

The detective's name was Holmes.* No comment. Percy Mapleton was tracked down and sent for trial where he insisted it was the mysterious 'third man' in the carriage who was the attacker. When the jury found Percy guilty he cried, 'The day will come when you shall know that you murdered me.'

The appeal on his behalf was novel … and you may like to make a note of it in case you are charged with murder. He said, 'I also murdered a lieutenant at Chatham Barracks in February. I must be mad.'

As Oscar Wilde didn't say, 'To kill one man is a misfortune, to kill two you must be bonkers.'

Foul for a farmer

'Never apologize, mister, it's a sign of weakness.'

John Wayne, American actor, as Nathan Brittles in movie She Wore a Yellow Ribbon *(1949)*

As Victoria lay dying in February 1901 a murder most foul happened on a train from Southampton to Waterloo. George Parker, a desperate unemployed marine, shot at Mrs Rhoda

---

* The inspector in charge also bore a famous name in criminal history – he was Inspector Turpin. The corpse was viewed in the stables of the Railway Tavern but we don't know if Black Bess was present. In another historic connection the police surgeon officiated over Jack the Ripper murders seven years later.

King and wounded her. His second bullet struck farmer William Pearson in the forehead and killed him.

Parker proceeded to rob the dead farmer as Mrs King sat bleeding.

People in stressed situations say and do some odd things. Killer Parker apologized to Mrs King: 'I'm sorry I shot you. I didn't mean to hurt you.'

Uh? I didn't mean to *hurt* you? So what did you mean, she must have wondered, sending a lead projectile towards me at several hundred miles per hour, Mr Parker?

His bullet entered her left cheek and broke her jaw … but he didn't *mean* to hurt her?

The wounded woman stayed calm and advised the killer to throw the gun out of the window. But the train was travelling slowly and workmen at the line side would have witnessed the act. She advised him to wait till he got to the next station, Vauxhall.

As he ran from the train she screamed a warning to the station staff; the unarmed man was caught by a policeman on traffic duty.

Parker's explanation was bizarre. He said he'd bought the pistol to shoot an ex-girlfriend who had spent all his money on riotous living. Shooting farmer Pearson was done 'on the spur of the moment'.

He was hanged. If only he'd finished off Mrs King and silenced her, instead of apologizing, he may have escaped.

First for females

It may seem that all of these hanged men suggest you simply cannot get away with murder on a train. Yet the killer of the first woman to die violently was never traced. A killer roaming free is a frightful thought.

> 'Where justice is denied, neither persons nor property
> will be safe.'
>
> *Frederick Douglass (1818–95), African/American social reformer*

On a February evening in 1897 Miss Elizabeth Camp climbed aboard a stopping train from Hounslow. She met her Waterloo on the train and never reached Waterloo alive. She was found in a second-class compartment with her skull crushed. The murder weapon was found at the trackside between Putney and Wandsworth. It was a bloodied pestle – the sort used to grind spices or drugs in a mortar.

Whodunnit? A mad scientist perhaps, running amok with his pulverizing pestle, his burning Bunsen and his terrifying test-tubes?

The police tracked down a young man with bandaged hands seen leaving the train … but he'd hurt his hands fixing a bicycle – he may have been a frequenter of cycle-paths but he was no psychopath.

Detectives said they suspected that old Victorian standby, a 'wandering lunatic' … but no mad murderer was ever traced. The lunatic must have wandered off back to Buckingham Palace or Wonderland like Jack the Ripper had nine years before.*

And, like Jack or Jill the Ripper, the perpetrator was never caught and the crime never solved, though there was a list of suspects as long as a cut-throat razor. We are simply left with the wise words of poor Elizabeth's sister, who'd cautioned the

---

* Jack the Ripper suspects included Queen Victoria's grandson, the Duke of Clarence (driven mad by syphilis). Also accused is *Alice in Wonderland* author Lewis Carroll. Carroll was a children's author so he must have been mad by definition.

victim before she climbed into her carriage ... 'Third class is safer for women.'*

Elizabeth should have listened. She was the first woman to be murdered on the railways and, at the age of 33, that is not what you want as your memorial.

Terrorist targets

In the 1880s the Irish independence group, the Fenians, organized a dynamite campaign against the British rulers on the mainland. Establishment buildings like the Tower of London and Parliament were singled out. But the rail network was vulnerable to attack and the London Underground became a target.

In 1883 the first explosions occurred on the Metropolitan line in the evening rush hour, then ten minutes later on the District line. Flying glass caused the majority of the injuries. A victim said ...

> 'I heard an explosion like the report of a cannon. I saw a flash and the lights in the carriage went out suddenly. When I had collected myself I removed from my head a piece of glass about an inch and a half in length. I remembered no more.'
>
> *William George, passenger*

---

* Third class had been popular on the urban routes but took a long time to be accepted on the inter-city main lines. In 1872 the Midland Railway supplied third-class carriages on its express trains and there was outrage. Hamilton Ellis, Midland Railway historian, said, 'Some other companies considered that an express train was something for which travellers should be made to pay handsomely.' They still do.

In 1884 London's major stations were targeted with bags full of explosives and a timer deposited in left-luggage offices. Only the one at Victoria exploded. No one was arrested but clues pointed to American supporters of the Irish Fenians.

'I'm Irish. I think about death all the time.'

Jack Nicholson (1937—), American actor

In 1885 a bomb was detonated between Gower Street and King's Cross. A witness said …

'Several persons in the Euston road, in proximity to the gratings, were thrown off their feet while the horses of the omnibuses and other vehicles were restrained only with great difficulty from running away. Several women on the platform fainted.'

It's the corsets that did it.*

There were no deaths and a letter to *The Times* mocked the bombers as 'cowardly scoundrels' and 'failures'. But the terrorists had brought terror to the streets of London.†
Like Guy Fawkes before them, the 'failures' had made their point.‡

Eventually an Irish-American man was arrested, tried and convicted of treason. He was sentenced to life imprison-

---

* I mean it's the corsets that made the ladies faint. Not the corsets that threw the bombs. Don't be silly.

† The chief suspect was said to be a man in a fur-collared coat and a 'wide-awake' hat. How did the hat get its name? It was a joke. The wide-awake hat was so named because the hat felt does not have a nap. Apologies if your sides split laughing at that Victorian humour.

‡ There had been a police corruption scandal in 1877 and one theory was that certain police officers carried out the bombing to frighten the public into loving the bluebottles.

ment with hard labour. The 'cowardly scoundrel' was just 22 years old.*****

His mistake was to throw the bomb from an underground train window when the guard of the train in question was an ex-policeman.

Stupid staff

Railway staff could cause frightening explosions without the aid of dynamiters. On a dark October morning 1869 there were complaints of a smell of gas at Newton Abbot station's waiting room. Mr Hemmett, the station's inspector, investigated.

It was dark. So he had to look for the leak with an oil lamp, didn't he? Criminal.

> 'He had just about enough intelligence to open
> his mouth when he wanted to eat, but certainly
> no more.'
>
> *P. G. Wodehouse (1881–1975), English author*

Mr Hemmett was injured. No one else was hurt. It's hard to feel sorry for him.

---

* Shehzad Tanweer was also aged 22 when he detonated a suicide bomb aboard a tube train travelling between Liverpool Street and Aldgate stations on 7 July 2005. Two of his fellow bombers were aged 19 and 18. There were 52 deaths and 700 injuries.

— THE POLICEMAN'S FRIEND —

Railways didn't just generate crime. They also helped catch criminals. In 1843, in Slough, John Tawell put cyanide in an ex-girlfriend's ale. Then he headed for his getaway vehicle – the next train to Paddington. Her screams alerted the public and he was followed to the station, where the railway staff telegraphed ahead to the London police.

Tawell was arrested at Paddington. His final journey would be from the condemned cell to the gallows.

||||||||||||||||||||||||||||||||||||||||||||||||||||||||||||||||||||||||||||||||||||||||||||||||||||||||

BRIEF TIMELINE – THE SIXTIES

||||||||||||||||||||||||||||||||||||||||||||||||||||||||||||||||||||||||||||||||||||||||||||||||||||||||

1860   Trains are taking people to the seaside and resorts are growing. To feed the flocking trippers the fish-and-chip shop is invented.

1861   America breaks out in Civil War while Mrs Beeton produces a civilized cook book in Britain. Prince Albert dies. Queen Vic mourns – for 40 years.

1863   London Underground Railway opens. 12,000 people have been displaced … and quite a few corpses from cemeteries. A Football Association compiles a set of laws for the game.*

———

* The rules say players ARE allowed to 'hack the front of the leg' of an opponent. Many believe that charging, hacking and tripping are an important part of the game. One supporter of hacking said that without it 'You will do away with the courage and pluck of the game, and it will be bound to bring over a lot of Frenchmen who would beat you with a week's practice.' (That'll never happen.)

1864   Isambard Brunel's Clifton suspension bridge opens but he doesn't enjoy the success since he's been dead five years. Cardiff Docks open; now the railways can bring coal from the valleys. The little town has a capital future.

1865   Charles Dickens survives the Staplehurst Rail crash. He's a hero for helping the injured and dying – not to mention rescuing the latest chapter of his novel. But he is hiding a scandalous secret.

1866   Manchester death rates reach 40 per 1,000 because of the filth. But Dr John Snow is cracking the cholera problem by spotting the problem lies in the water. The second 'Railway Mania' bubble bursts.

1867   Alfred Nobel demonstrates his explosive new invention. No prizes for guessing it's dynamite. It will change tunnelling for Britain's railways but not really reduce the deaths and dangers. Thomas Barnardo opens his Mission for Destitute Children.

1868   Trains have been non-smoking but Parliament passes a law forcing every train to have a smoking compartment. British trains won't be smoke-free again till 2005.

1870   Charles Dickens dies, 'exhausted by fame' and traumatized by his rail-crash experience.

FAILURE AND FIRE

⚊ BUBBLE BACK ⚊

The calendars turned to the 1860s and memories of the ruinous Railway Mania of the 1840s were fading. A new generation was waiting to prove history wrong and create a second railway bubble. A bubble, they said wisely, that wouldn't burst … of course.

> 'History is the most cruel of goddesses. She leads her triumphal car over heaps of corpses, not only in war but in "peaceful" economic developments.'
>
> *Friedrich Engels (1820–95), German social scientist*

Engels may have had Railway Mania in mind when he wrote that. There were certainly heaps of corpses for the goddess History to roll over when, surprise of surprises, this second bubble burst in 1866. This time the overambitious rail schemes collapsed in a rubble of debt and managed to bring down a few banks with them.

The public panicked in an effort to grab their gold before the banks ran out.*

---

* Just as they did in 2007 when Northern Rock hinted it may be in trouble. Savers got their money; shareholders lost theirs.

> 'Don't gamble; take all your savings and buy some
> good stock and hold it till it goes up, then sell it.
> If it don't go up, don't buy it.'
>
> *Will Rogers (1879–1935), American cowboy and humorist*

By 1860 most of the major lines had been built. Now the people (and the businesses) of Britain were clamouring to be joined to the main rail grid. This was the age of the branch railway. Even the branches grew branches … or twigs perhaps? These branches would invariably prove to be unprofitable and in need of pruning (as that master tree-surgeon Dr Beeching was to assert a hundred years later).

— HARSH LESSONS —

It wasn't only investors who faced dangerous days where the railways were concerned.

The Railway Mania (or train-ia) drove technology. Trains became faster and the companies competed like Olympians to be 'Faster, Higher, Stronger' than the opposition. Even if it meant taking risks.

> 'Competition is the keen cutting edge of business,
> always shaving away at costs.' *
>
> *Henry Ford (1863–1947), American industrialist*

---

* And one of the highest 'costs' is wages. Your workers may not agree your aims are all that laudable, Mr Ford, but you'd be worth a couple of hundred billion dollars by today's standards so who are we to cavil, carp or complain about your advice?

'Man cannot discover new oceans unless he has the
courage to lose sight of the shore.'

André Gide (1869–1951), French author

So many projects, so few experienced engineers. The result?
Inexperienced engineers, builders and railway operators.
A classic example was the Ashton-under-Lyne viaduct in
1845. Navvies laughed when they were told about a crack in
a near-complete railway viaduct. Then the nine arches collapsed like dominoes. Fifteen would never laugh again.

Experts said the mortar simply wasn't holding the
masonry together. A coroner's jury said there was negligence
on the part of the contractors … but returned a verdict of
'accidental' death.

Bad design and careless workmanship? An accident?
Obviously no compensation culture in those days. No one
gurning and grinning at you from an advert as they rub
their hands and ask, 'Had an accident at work that wasn't
your fault? We're here to help you get the compensation you
deserve. No win no fee.' Those ambulance-chasers would
have had a field day on Victoria's railways.

The work was delayed three months but then went on, the
viaduct rebuilt. Lesson learned – at a cost.

'I am always doing that which I cannot do, in order
that I may learn how to do it.' *

Pablo Picasso

---

* Mr P. was not renowned for building bridges with some penny-
pinching contractor's cost-cutting, sub-standard materials. He took risks
at the easel … easily.

There is a theory that accidents are 'good', because we learn from them …

> 'Failure saves lives. In the airline industry, every time a plane crashes the probability of the next crash is lowered by that. The *Titanic* saved lives because we're building bigger and bigger ships. So these people died, but we have effectively improved the safety of the system, and nothing failed in vain.'
>
> *Nassim Nicholas Taleb (1960—), Lebanese American essayist*

Of course this is no consolation if you are too dead to learn the lesson. What sort of person would happily say, 'I am happy to die so that others might live'? All right, Jesus might say that, and a few holders of the Victoria Cross, but most of us would rather do without accidents. Not many of us would relish being crucified for our fellow humans … or being burned to death.

> 'My Dad used to say "always fight fire with fire", which is probably why he got thrown out of the fire brigade.'
>
> *Peter Kay (1973—), English comedian*

The trouble with pushing back the boundaries of knowledge is mistakes are made and often paid for with human lives. Trains are one of the most lethal weapons in the world – tons of metal travelling at high speeds with long stopping distances. When the L&MR was opened there was still a lot to learn – and a lot of people who died in the classroom of steam and iron and scalding water. The railways needed rules.

> 'I am quite sure some interference on the part of the
> government is much wanted. I am convinced that
> some system should be laid down to prevent wild
> and visionary schemes being tried, to great danger of
> injury or loss of life to the public.'
>
> *George Stephenson, letter to the Board of Trade, 1841* *

So what were these lessons that needed to be learned?

➢ **Tracks** George Stephenson had never built a twin-tracked railway before the L&MR. He had established the space between the rails was 4 foot 8½ inches. But what should be the space between the two tracks? Oh hang it, let's make it the same, he thought. It turned out that was too small, because the coaches overhung the track and left little space for trains to pass. That was one of the factors in the death of William Huskisson. If you end up on a railway line you should be able to stand between the tracks and the onrushing trains would miss you. A life-saving lesson.

➢ **Corridors** No one had the idea of carriages with a corridor joining them. So a train guard would have to check tickets by walking along the step-boards outside of the carriages and punch tickets through the carriage windows.† Thomas Port was a guard on the Euston train

---

* Incidentally, Geordie added a revealing sentence: 'Perhaps I ought to be the last man to admit this (the whole system of Railways and Locomotives having been brought out by my own exertions).' George Stephenson has wrongly been called the 'Father of the Railways' and the 'Father of the Locomotive'. His apologists say, 'But he never called himself that.' So what is that sentence if it's not a boast of being Father of everything rail-related? Hoist by your own petard, Geordie.

† Railway guards obsessed about second-class passengers sneaking into first-class compartments, they still do. They just don't take the obsession so far as to walk along the outside of the carriage.

to Birmingham and set off along the step-boards. The tricky bit was crossing from one carriage to the next. He slipped and fell under the wheels. The doctors amputated his legs (without an anaesthetic) but he died from loss of blood. His gravestone in Harrow-on-the-Hill is a gruesome reminder of how useful corridors are …

> To the memory of
> Thomas Port who near this town had both his legs
> Severed from his body by the railway train.
> With the greatest fortitude he bore a
> Second amputation by the surgeons, and
> Died from loss of blood.
> August 7th 1838 aged 33 years.
>
> *Bright rose the morn, and vigorous rose poor Port.*
> *Gay on the Train he used his wonted sport:*
> *Ere noon arrived his mangled form they bore,*
> *With pain distorted and o'erwhelmed with gore:*
> *When evening came to close the fatal day,*
> *A mutilated corpse the sufferer lay.* *

➢ **Windows** Early carriages had no glass in the windows so the clothes of the passengers were in danger of being singed by cinders and holed by hot sparks. Their hair could become a holocaust of the head. Eventually windows were fitted – in first class first, as you'd expect. But a window that opens has always been a temptation and a danger on a train journey. In 1845 railway engineer Jan Perner was making a triumphal return from

---

* As with most epitaphs this one must have offered so much comfort to the wife and two children as they laid their flowers on the grave.

the opening of the 100 km Prague to Pardubice railway he had designed and overseen. He stuck his head out of a carriage window and it was struck by a careless passing pole. He died the next day.

> 'Never underestimate the power of human stupidity.'
> *Robert A. Heinlein (1907–88), American sci-fi writer*

➤ **Signals** There were no signals on the first railway tracks. Instead there was a policeman who would time the trains. If the last train had passed through less than ten minutes before, he would stop the next train. If the train broke down he would have to run to the end and stop following trains … a bit like Bobby in *The Railway Children*, but without the red petticoats. A driver was instructed to build a coal fire in the middle of the track to give advance warning to following trains. Smoke signals in fact.* But if a signalman left it till the last moment to set a red for danger it could be too late.

> SIGNALMAN:　　　　'Can I stick me signals up?'
> WILLIAM PORTER:　'Yes, if it'll give you any pleasure.'
> *Will Hay as 'William Porter' in movie* Oh, Mr Porter! *(1937)*

When signals were designed they showed a white light meaning the line was clear. Only when there was danger did the signalman switch to red for danger. The peril of this practice was demonstrated in 1876 when a snowstorm swept across the east coast line. Just south

---

* Smoke signals were invented by the Ancient Chinese soldiers on the Great Wall. Not a lot of people know that. You do now.

of Peterborough a slow goods train failed to see the warning signals and chugged on in the path of the London express. They collided and fell onto the north-bound track. A northbound express smashed into the wreckage. Fourteen people died. The signalmen (still called policemen) had all the signals set to red for danger. So what went wrong? The snow had clogged the signals and they were stuck on white for clear. The default should have been red. It was later changed. The crash investigator put it in dramatic prose ...

'The most subtle ingenuity could hardly devise a means more misleading, or more certain of success, for luring the engine drivers with their precious human freight, forward to inevitable destruction.'

Captain Tyler – Abbots Ripton disaster report

But human error often played its part ...

At Bo'ness in 1862 a dozy signalman/policeman had confused two express trains – one from Perth, one from Glasgow – and believed the line was clear. He allowed a goods train to shunt trucks onto the main line. At the last moment he remembered the second express was due. He threw the signal to red to stop the onrushing express. The express driver's last words said it all ...

'Brakes! Brakes! That is a red, but it's too late.'

Driver Robert Allen to fireman ✱

✱ Unfortunately the train was travelling with its tender first. The impact sent the coals cascading onto the driver and they pinned him to the red-hot firebox. Frying tonight.

Railway policemen were also responsible for setting ...

➤ **Points** Get it wrong and a train could be derailed. At St Helens two locomotives were routed to collide head on after a policeman on point duty made a mistake. A driver was killed. The policemen who dozed off were a danger to everyone. Nowadays we use sleeping police-men to make our travel *safer*. Ironic.

➤ **Shunting** In 1848 a locomotive shunted across points at Conwy station, but left its last carriage overhanging the main line. A main-line train struck it, the carriage was shattered and a VIP passenger staggered out and collapsed from the shock. He was Robert Stephenson and he was on his way back from the funeral of his father just days before. Two legendary Stephensons dead within a week ... and the second from a train acci-dent? The ultimate irony. But Robert survived.

Did you know ... losing on points

A train to Carlisle was diverted into a siding by a careless labourer who had set the points incorrectly. In spite of the driver throwing the engine into reverse it skidded down an incline onto a loading platform and tumbled three metres to the roadway below. It landed on the back of a cart that was being loaded. A workman was killed. When the debris was cleared it was discov-ered that two boys aged 14 and 16 had stowed away for a free ride under the cart. It was reported that the head of John Kelsay, one of the boys '... was crushed quite flat, and presented a frightful spectacle'.

➤ **Doors** Following Huskisson's misadventure, a passenger wrote to suggest doors that opened inwards. Awkward. Passengers were too fond of getting out to stretch their legs on long journeys – or jumping on or off at unauthorized times. The answer? Have the guard come along and lock all the doors before the train set off. In 1836 a broken axle sent a carriage tumbling down an embankment – with passengers as trapped as baked beans in a can. Luckily the coach didn't catch fire and turn them into baked beings … and amazingly no one was seriously hurt. But imprisoning passengers would eventually be banned.

➤ **Couplings** Locos and coaches were joined by chains. As the locomotive accelerated and decelerated the crashing of coach on coach was jarring … but not dangerous? A young fireman was sent to uncouple truck chains. The primitive hand-signals didn't save him when two trucks came together. His head was crushed and he suffered train-chain brain-drain damage.

➤ **Clocks** Nowadays there is Greenwich Mean Time for all. But until the 1850s each town had its own 'local time'. That caused some chaos. In 1840 an inspector had suggested everyone run on 'London Time' but it took some years for the idea to be universally adopted.✽ By 1855 only 90 per cent of railways had complied and many local people objected to losing their own clock

---

✽ And just when you thought it was safe to get back on the trains there was a crash at Tamworth Station. Everyone was on London time so why did the signalman get his timing wrong and divert the Irish Mail Express through a siding and into the River Tame? Because his watch stopped. Oooops.

setting. In 1849 a train set off from Bootle in Lancashire but stalled in a tunnel. Not a problem. The guard had to run back and leave warning detonators on the line as a danger signal to a following train.* The second train should have been ten minutes behind … or so the guard thought. No rush. The second train arrived after just three minutes and smashed into the back of the stalled one. Why? Because each was running on a different 'local time'. And even if a following train saw a warning there was a danger it couldn't stop in time because they had inefficient …

➢ **Brakes** Trains DID have brakes but they weren't very good. A trial (like the Rainhill Trial in reverse) was held at Newark in 1875 to find the brake system that could stop the quickest. Vacuum brakes won – 48 years after William Huskisson was run over by the unstoppable *Rocket*. In 1878 a law was passed that forced companies to fit vacuum brakes to all their coaches. A deadly delay.

➢ **Whistles** In 1833 on the Leicester and Swannington Railway, a Robert Stephenson loco called *Samson* collided with a horse and cart loaded with butter and eggs. They were scrambled. The engine had a horn but it seems it wasn't loud enough. The line manager, Mr Bagster, suggested the engines should be fitted with steam whistles. Progress.

---

* A dodgy occupation. A stalled train often found some steam and pulled away leaving the guard behind, probably crying, 'Stop that train!' while waving a red petticoat.

➤   **Food** Before the days of buffet cars passengers were obliged to get off at stations to refresh themselves. The eating and (especially) the drinking delayed services and cost the directors money. A criminal delay to the money-men …

> 'It is an inconvenience and a nuisance from the hawking of Eccles Cakes and Ale to railway passengers at almost every stopping place between Warrington Junction and Manchester.'
>
> *Minutes of L&MR board meeting*

Who'd have thought Eccles cakes would be responsible for such anti-social behaviour? Food on Victorian Railways was widely condemned.

> 'The real disgrace of England is the railway sandwich – that whitened sepulchre, fair enough outside, but so meagre, poor and spiritless within.'
>
> *Anthony Trollope (1815–82), English author*

‑ FIRE ON THE TRACKS ‑

> 'Never take a wife till thou hast a house (and a fire)
> to put her in.'
>
> *Benjamin Franklin*

The fear of fire is a primeval one. Coal and flying sparks could turn wooden coaches to kindling.

Round Oak disaster 1858

> 'The problem with drinking and driving is …
> The MOURNING after!'
>
> *American drink-driving campaign slogan*

The Wolverhampton to Worcester excursion train was meant to be a treat for the children. But the train was packed with adults … who had the minds of two-year-olds.

The partying parasites were particularly prevalent in the guard's van, where Guard Cook was mein host. The drink flowed. The party game of choice was to spin his screw brake and make the long train judder. This was such a fun game the revellers broke the coupling chains three times before the train reached Worcester. The repairs Cook made at Worcester were patchy.

On the return journey the train pulled up at Round Oak and the coupling chain snapped again. This time the guard's van set off down a steady gradient – along with 17 carriages and 450 passengers. Gathering pace as it went, it hurtled downhill towards the following train.

'Jump! Jump! Or we'll all be killed,' Guard Cook cried …

then jumped and saved his own skin. It did no good for the passengers: 14 died and 50 were badly injured.

Cook was questioned at the inquiry. 'It was the driver's jerky stop that snapped the coupling chain. I screwed the brake down but the hill was too steep, the carriages too heavy. I could do nothing.'

He was lying. The accident inspector bravely tested Cook's claims. He allowed a train with 17 carriages and a guard's van to run back down that hill. He applied the brake. The carriages stopped safely. (Brave man to risk his life.) The wrecked brake van showed the brake was *off*.

Cook was proved a liar. 'Gravity' was found not guilty.

The real villains were the railway company that allowed a children's treat tour to degenerate into a booze-fest and, of course, the reckless, feckless drinkers.

||||||||||||||||||||||||||||||||||||||||||||||||||||||||||||||||||||||||||||||||||||||||||||||||||||||

BRIEF TIMELINE – THE SEVENTIES

||||||||||||||||||||||||||||||||||||||||||||||||||||||||||||||||||||||||||||||||||||||||||||||||||||||

1871   Henry Stanley 'discovers' Dr David Livingstone in Africa, even though the Scottish missionary didn't know he'd been lost.* Bank Holidays invented and the train excursions can make day-trips to exotic places like Blackpool viable. Rock on.

1872   The first FA Cup Final held and trains are essential in getting fans there ... ex-public schoolboy team, Wanderers, won. Later that year the first international between England and Scotland, which they drew.

---

* Stanley's greeting is famously remembered as, 'Dr Livingstone, I presume.' Livingstone's reply is famously forgotten. He replied, 'Yes.' Which is a polite way of saying, 'Well I'm not a red-bottomed baboon, you Welsh wazzock.'

1873   Sleeping-car service introduced on the London and
        Glasgow overnight train … but you have to bring
        your own bed linen.

1874   Belgian aviator, Vincent de Groof, dies when his
        balloon crashes into a Chelsea street.

1875   Matthew Webb becomes the first person to swim
        the English Channel. He probably missed the boat
        train.

1876   Alexander Graham Bell makes the first phone
        call.* He says, 'Watson come here, I need you.'
        (No it was not Sherlock Holmes making the
        elementary request.)

1877   Victoria is proclaimed Empress of India, whether
        the Indians want her or not. Two hundred people
        travel by rail and bike to watch the first lawn
        tennis championships at a little suburb called
        Wimbledon. Spencer Gore wins.

1879   The Tay Bridge disaster brings gloom to the
        railways. Joseph Swan's electric light, demonstrated
        in Newcastle, will bring brightness to the world
        and eventually light-pollution.

The Abergele rail disaster, 1868

'O! for a muse of fire, that would ascend the brightest
heaven of invention.'

William Shakespeare

---

* On a device originally conceived as a hearing aid. Bet you didn't know
that.

Fire is a useful marvel of the universe – we all know the quote about it being a good servant but a bad master. Gravity is another handy wonder to have around. Australians would fall off the bottom of the planet if we didn't have it. But again we have to handle its forces with care.

Mishandle *both* gravity and fire and what do you have? The Abergele rail disaster.

Abergele lies on the north coast of Wales. In 1868 it was the scene of the worst railway crash yet in Britain, and also the most alarming.

> 'Goods trains, when likely to be overtaken by a passenger train, must be shunted at least ten minutes before the passenger train is due.'
>
> *London and North-Western Company rules*

A sensible precaution. The stationmaster ignored it and allowed a goods train to shunt on the main line at Llysfaen. The Irish Mail was due in less than ten minutes. A careless brakesman failed to apply the brakes on the goods train and it ran off, down the main line towards Abergele.

Arthur Thompson, the engine driver of the Irish Mail, saw the runaway wagons no more than 200 yards in front. He shut off steam. The fireman, who had also seen the hazard, applied his brake. Thompson then prepared to jump off and called to his fireman, 'For God's sake, Joe, jump! We can do no more.'* Thompson jumped; his fireman did not. Thompson heard his mate's despairing cry, the thunderous collision, but no other human sound.

The Irish Mail had its engine, tender and leading guard's

---

* You can see a pattern emerging, can't you? 'Oooops! We're going to crash. Save yourself and sod the passengers.'

van derailed. The locomotive ran on about 30 yards and overturned to the left; the tender overturned to the right and ended up fouling the other line. A returning Irish Mail train was due to arrive shortly.

What made the Abergele derailment so disastrous? The fact that the runaway goods' wagons were carrying 50 wooden barrels holding a total of 1,700 gallons (8,000 litres) of paraffin oil.

The overturned engine scattered its hot ashes over the paraffin from the shattered barrels.

As the *Railway News* reported …

'No other collision has ever yet, in this country at least, been attended with such a loss of life, nor presented such horrifying features. The crashing of the engine and carriages into a heap of splinters, each of which wounds unfortunate passengers like a sword, is horrible enough to contemplate; but when fire in its fiercest form is added to the scene, no more frightful occurrence could be imagined.'

The flaming liquid, like a napalm strike, smothered the wooden carriages at the front of the mail train. The doors to each compartment were locked. A literal Hell.

There were 32 passengers inside. Not one survived. The accident investigator reported later …

'They can only be described as charred pieces of flesh and bone.'

Colonel Rich report (1868)

The victims were found to be burnt beyond recognition. Three of them were later identified by their personal effects. The remains of Lord Farnham were identified by the crest engraved on his watch. A statue to his memory now stands outside the new Johnston Central Library on Farnham Street in Cavan Town.*

DANGEROUS DAYS DEATH VII

FIRE

Victim: Lord Farnham

Smoke rapidly fills the compartment and you have nothing else to breathe but the thick, acrid smoke.

Yours eyes sting and water horribly but this is nothing compared to the irritation of the smoke in your windpipe and lungs, causing you to cough violently. The superheated gases burn your respiratory lining, removing all those troublesome nasal hairs, but destroying the vital oxygen-transferring system in the process, leaving you only deadly gases like carbon monoxide and cyanide to breathe.

Unable to get any oxygen to your brain, you lose consciousness. Your clothing and hair burst into flames, skin blisters and cracks, underlying fat bubbles and blackens as you cook very quickly in the six minutes your brain takes to die.

Dr Peter Fox

'Some say the world will end in fire, some say in ice.'
Robert Frost (1874–1963), American poet †

---

* We have to hope and assume that the statue represents him before he was reduced to charred pieces of flesh and bone.

† Neither one is a very pleasant prospect to contemplate … but we can guess which one Mr Frost will be putting his money on.

The Armagh disaster, 1889

It was a simple sort of accident in Northern Ireland.

A 15-coach excursion train, packed with 940 passengers. They included 600 children, on a Sunday school trip to the seaside.

The God-fearing even wrote hymns that used the metaphor of God inviting you aboard His 'Railway to Heaven' …

> 'O! What a deal we hear and read
> About railways and railway speed,
> Of lines which are, or may be made;
> And selling shares is quite a trade.
> Jesus is the first engineer,
> He does the gospel engine steer;
> "My son," says God, "give me thy heart;
> Make haste or else the train will start."'*
>
> A Month in Yorkshire *(1858) by Walter White, English travel writer*

Were the 600 Sunday school children singing 'The Railway to Heaven' not knowing it was about to become the Railway to Hell?

The train left Armagh and set off up an incline. The driver, unfamiliar with the line, found he hadn't enough power to climb the hill from Armagh. As he almost reached the summit at Dobbin's Bridge he ran out of steam – the more facetious may say he ran out of horse-power. (Dobbin … horse … oh, never mind.)

---

* It's good to know God speaks English. He still has a bit to learn about making his lyrics scan. A lot to learn. And you have to wonder who delivered his coal?

The crew decided to take the front five coaches over the hill, park them in a siding and come back for the remaining ten, which would be left on the main line.

The driver uncoupled the back carriages, but it was a vacuum-brake system. Break the train and you lose the vacuum.

The driver was setting away with the front five carriages but allowed the train to roll back … like a novice learner driver in a car attempting a hill start. The front of the train gave the rear section a crack that drove it over the stones used to chock the wheels.

Our old friend 'Gravity' took over and despite the crew's best efforts* the detached rear carriages began to roll back towards Armagh. It met the following passenger train at speed. The first three runaway carriages disintegrated and the others were thrown down the embankment. Eighty died and as many again were injured. About a third of the victims were children.

The irony? If the excursion driver had waited, that following train could have pushed the children's train safely over the crest of the hill.

A law was passed to ensure that changes were made to the vacuum system.† Thereafter the railways were a safer place for passengers.

---

* I say 'best efforts' but there was some panic. As they attempted to reconnect the train they tripped over old rails lying by the track. It never occurred to them to use those rails to put a spoke in the runaway wheels. They just put stones on the track which were quickly crushed to sand under the packed carriages.

† The more modern (intelligent) brake design known as 'continuous brakes' *applied* the brakes when the vacuum was broken – known as a 'fail-safe' system. This train was the old system, where the opposite happened and disconnection *released* the brakes. A sort of 'fail-and-you're dead' system. 'Continuous braking' was enforced by law after this disaster.

> 'It's fine to celebrate success but it is more important
> to heed the lessons of failure.'
>
> *Bill Gates (1955—), American business magnate*

Norton Fitzwarren disaster, 1890

Norton Fitzwarren is a place on the Great Western rail line
… it is not the father of Dick Whittington's lover, Alice Fitzwarren. The villain of the disaster pantomime was George
Rice.

You can understand why George would be prone to the
human error that led to ten fatalities. He was a signalman …
alone in his lonely box, through a freezing November night,
with dreams of a warm bed and a hearty breakfast to distract
him.

George moved a goods train onto the London line so a
fast train could bustle through to Devon. The driver of the
goods train saw the fast train go past and waited for the
signal to go.

And waited. And waited. He waited seven minutes. He
was stationary on the mail line to London … not a healthy
place to wait. His signalman cried the bad news, 'Here's a
train a-coming on our line and he's never going to stop.'

The train was a special, travelling light at a speed of 60
mph. It met the parked goods engine head on. The conse-
quences can be imagined.

The crews survived, but ten passengers died and nine
more were seriously hurt.

And the b-i-g question was, 'Why did George Rice signal
the fast train forward when the goods train was parked on
its line?'

Because he forgot. (We assume he remembered when he saw the mangled results of his mistake.)

> 'He looked haggard and careworn, like a Borgia who has suddenly remembered that he has forgotten to shove cyanide in the consommé, and the dinner-gong due any moment.'
>
> *P. G. Wodehouse,* Carry on, Jeeves

George tried to explain his tragic amnesia … he'd been knocked over by a train ten months before and never been right since. 'I'd been bad in the head all night,' he muttered.

The sleeping sentry

> 'Grim death took me without any warning
> I was well at night, and died in the morning.'
>
> *Gravestone epitaph, Sevenoaks, Kent*

Tired signal operators could be lethal. Just two years after the Norton Fitzwarren accident Signalman James Holmes had been nursing a sick child and had no sleep. Next morning he went in a futile search for a doctor but returned to find the child dead. Holmes pleaded to be relieved of his duty at Manor House (Thirsk, between York and Darlington), that night. No relief could be found, so grieving James was obliged to do the night shift.

He fell asleep at the critical moment when a goods train entered his section ahead of an express. He should have signalled the express to stop.

When the express slammed into the back of the goods train the Pullman sleeping car shot off its wheel and crunched the third-class carriage ahead.

In that carriage 8 died and 39 were injured. How many died in the first-class Pullman? Not one. Which says a lot about the quality lavished on the rich traveller as opposed to the poor. These days the difference in class on the East Coast line is a matter of free wine and sandwiches. In the 1890s it was simply a matter of life and death.

'Privilege is the greatest enemy of right.'
Marie von Ebner-Eschenbach (1830–1916), Austrian writer

James Holmes was charged with manslaughter and found guilty. But his situation aroused so much sympathy the judge set him free – a decision that was greeted with a warm wave of cheering in court.

The result was a reduction in the hours that signalmen worked and a better system of relief when a man was unfit for duty.

POVERTY
AND PLAGUE

> MR TRIMBLETOW: 'There's a place in Ireland called
>   Buggleskelly.' *
> WILLIAM PORTER: 'That's nothing, there's a place in
>   Wales called Llanfairpwllgwyngyllgogerychwyrn-
>   drobwllllantysiliogogogoch.'
>
> *From movie* Oh, Mr Porter!

B y the 1870s the railways were as normal a part of Victorian life as shoving little boys up chimneys had been a hundred years before. Soot-stained stations were crowded with commuters complaining about tardy trains. No one looked at the blackened bricks and wondered what the smoke was doing to their lungs.† In the 1830s rail travel had been a magic carpet ride …

---

* The writer of the movie script was being facetious. Why not go for a real Irish place name? Perhaps Ballydehob on the Schull and Skibereen line? Or did he think Ballydehob too exotic?
† It's the 'romance' of steam, isn't it? Train-spotters forget about the effects of passive smoking as they wallow in the glamour of the grey grit from the chuffing chimneys.

'The whirl through the confused darkness on those steam wings, was one of the strangest things I have ever experienced – hissing and dashing on, we knew not whither. We saw gleams of towns in the distance – unknown towns. We went over the tops of houses – one town I saw clearly with its chimney heads vainly stretching up towards us – under the stars; not under the clouds but among them. We flew … as if some huge, steam night-bird had flung you on its back.'

Thomas Carlyle, letter, 1839

By the 1870s rail journeys had become commonplace.

While the occasional spectacular disaster shook the public from their complacency, the quiet deaths of the workers carried on unnoticed. Between 1874 and 1879 an average of 682 railway workers a year died with their boots on. That is almost two a day.

William Huskisson, run over by *Rocket,* had been remembered with processions and plaques and orations and obituaries. The 3,410 railway employees who died 1874–9 had only the tears of their families and a pitiful plot in their churchyard to mark their loss.

Did you know … shunting

The most dangerous occupation in Victorian Britain was not being a miner or a mill worker or a sweep, it was being a railway shunter. Being crushed between wagons was common. Stepping onto the main line at the wrong time would be fatal. In India the shunting accident rate was lower because the railways often used elephants to shunt trucks. They probably knew exactly when the next express was due because an elephant never forgets.

Many of the victims were the railway builders, of course. Tunnels fall on you as you build them. Or you fall off bridges as you build them. You tumble off embankments or cuttings collapse onto you.

> 'We call it the slaughterhouse because, you know, every day nearly there's an accident and nigh every week a death. I stood and looked down and there were the chaps ever so far below and the cutting so narrow. And a lot of stone fell. There was no room to get away and mostly no warning.'
>
> *Navvy interview related to Elizabeth Garnett in her book*
> Our Navvies *(1885)*

In the dangerous days on Victoria's railways there seemed to be no safe job.

— THE NAVVIES' GRAVEYARDS —

The railways rolled across the map of Britain like slug trails over a pavement. Contractors raced to hit deadlines rather than incur financial penalties. So safety was not exactly a priority. Workers routinely faced danger, miserable conditions, and disease. Including the killer disease: smallpox.

> 'I have seen men with smallpox thick upon them wandering about the lanes, having no place of shelter to go into.'
>
> *Robert Rawlinson, engineer to the Bridgewater Trust, 1845*

Between 1840 and 1850 around 50,000 bridges were built in Britain to accommodate the railways – more bridges than had existed in history till that time. That required an average of 300,000 bricks each.

Robert Stephenson needed large amounts for the Kilsby Tunnel (near Rugby) on the London and Birmingham Railway but the effort of transporting them would have been vast and expensive. The answer? Use the clay that was excavated from the tunnels to make the bricks on site.

> 'Erect a steam clay mill with kilns etc. sufficient to supply 30,000 bricks per day; say total quantity of bricks required 20,000,000 then 6,000,000 to be made from the open cuttings at the end of the tunnel.'
>
> *Robert Stephenson proposal, 1836*

Very green recycling scheme. And an expanded brick industry to provide work for thousands of unskilled workers. So unskilled, the brick industry was happy to use child labour.

In 1871 children were still being used in parts of the industry …

> 'I saw little children, three parts naked, tottering under the weight of wet clay, some of it on their heads, and some on their shoulders, and little girls with large masses of wet, cold and dripping clay pressing on their abdomens.'
>
> *Lord Shaftesbury (1801–85), politician and social reformer,*
> *report to the House of Lords, 1871*

Primitive? How about …

'A young boy is covered in soot from working at a brick-making kiln: Working children are a common sight at brickworks as they regularly employ entire families – who often make their homes on site.'

OR

'School is a luxury for the rural poor, with children often earning their keep as soon as they can walk.'

Where do these latter quotes come from? Another report from Lord Shaftesbury in 1871? No. A report from the *Daily Mail* newspaper in August 2013 describing conditions in modern Bangladesh. *Plus ça change, plus c'est la même chose* and all that. (Pardon my French.)

'The function of the historian is neither to love the past nor to emancipate himself from the past, but to master and understand it as the key to the understanding of the present.'

E. H. Carr (1892–1982), British historian

Boys would often be given the job of looking after the draft horses that pulled the wagons full of soil and rock away from the excavations. A healthy outdoor life, unlike that endured by the children who laboured underground in the coal mines? No, because they were subject to the same danger – slipping as the heavy wagons rolled relentlessly onward.

'A very young man, John Allen of the Western Railway, met with a frightful accident. A whole train of wagons went over his right arm and thigh, completely smashing both limbs. The loss of blood was so great that he died soon after.'

Felix Farley's Bristol Journal (1840)

'We heard stories that made one's blood curdle, of the cruelty of those from whom they rented the sties called dwellings. This, indeed, seems to us to be the great evil. Out of these wretches' health, comfort, and even lives, small capitalists reap a petty independence; and until the poor are rescued from the fangs of these mercenary men, there is but little hope either for their physical or moral welfare.'

Henry Mayhew, 'A Visit to the Cholera Districts of Bermondsey'

Patrick McGill was sold into slavery at about the age of 11. This was common at the time; poor Catholic families would sell a child to work for six or seven years as an agricultural labourer or maid. He wrote …

Down on creation's muck-pile where the sinful
      swelter and sweat,
Where the scum of the earth foregather, rough and
      untutored yet,
Where they swear in the six-foot places, or toil in the
      barrow squad,
The men of unshaven faces, the ranks of the very bad;

Patrick MacGill, 'The Song of the Shovel'

BRIEF TIMELINE – THE EIGHTIES

1880   First cricket test match in Britain sees England defeat Australia thanks to a cavalier 152 from young Dr W. G. Grace. Railway tunnelling under Lord's Cricket Ground is (graciously) suspended in the cricket season. Victorian children have suffered a lot but from now on they all have to attend school from 5 to 13, whether they want to or not. Man's inhumanity to children.

1883   The Dynamite Conspirators target public buildings and the underground railways. The Cheap Trains Act ensures affordable tickets for commuting workers.

1885   More competition for the railway when the 'safety bicycle' goes on sale. Safer than the penny-farthing predecessors anyway. Along with Dunlop's pneumatic rubber tyre, this will encourage a new cycling craze. PM Gladstone wants to see Irish Home Rule ... which may appease the dynamiters. But Parliament will reject it next year.

1886   Shop assistants under 18 are restricted to a maximum of 74 hours a week. Are you being served? Mr Benz creates the first petrol car. (It'll never catch on.)

1887   Queen Vic's golden jubilee – 30,000 children fed buns and milk in Hyde Park. Sherlock Holmes is created. Irish nationalist revolts in Trafalgar Square wound or kill 100. Bloody Sunday it's called ... not the last Sabbath to bear the name.

1888   Jack the Ripper brings fear (and blood) to the streets of London.

1889   Trains have helped migrate the rural workers
         to cities like London. But it's a mixed blessing.
         Of the 5.5 million people in the capital,
         one-third live in abject poverty.

The Ribblehead plague

'To the memory of those who through accidents lost
their lives in constructing the railway works between
Settle and Dent Head. This tablet was erected at the
joint expense of their fellow workmen and the
railway company, 1869 to 1876.'

Chapel-le-Dale graveyard memorial

By the late 1860s the great days of the railways were over. The main lines had all been built. But the Midland Railway wanted a new route to Scotland – one that would take them across the bleak moors and mountains of the North Pennines.

The Settle and Carlisle Railway line had been surveyed by a young engineer from Tasmania, Charles Sharland. He spent months in the desolate fells ... when he wasn't snowed in. The effort broke his health and he died before the work even started in 1869. The line's first victim never got to witness the human cost of his grand scheme.

Sharland had elected to cross a wide valley with the Ribblehead Viaduct. It cost on average one death a week and was to prove the final horror story for the navvy army.

First there was the horror of bog and boulder clay ...

➤ The sucking, squelching, sticking superglue of mud had a grip that could and did tear off a horse's hoof.

> ➤ Wheels sank in the mud so the barrows ran on barrels.
> ➤ At Ribbledale the clay was so hard it had to be blasted like rock.
> ➤ When the clay was soaked in the rain a navvy could sink a pick into it, but not pull it out again.

Add to that the horror of the weather and you have Misery. In 1872 alone 92 inches of rain fell at Dent Head on the line (compared to 25 inches in London that year).

Shanty towns of up to 2,000 workers and families sprang up. Rough places where the Sunday entertainment was bare-knuckle fighting. They named their towns after victories of the Crimean War, or (sarcastically) for posh districts of London, and Biblical names.

The missionaries who visited the camp would have to turn a blind eye to the usual navvy sins – poaching, fighting and rioting. Panicking police sought harsh punishments to deter the lawless. John Smith, aged 28, stole a pound in Kirkby Lonsdale. He was sentenced to 7 years' penal servitude. That's harsh.

The building of the Ribblehead Viaduct with its 24 arches was a massive achievement. The structure was a quarter-mile long and took four years to complete. But if we measure the cost in human lives it was enormous. Of course men fell from the mighty parapets. But a bigger killer lurked in the shanty shacks. The killer's name was smallpox.

Contractors tried to stem the spread of infection by isolating the victims. But one carter recalled …

'In three years I've toted over a hundred down the hill to the little churchyard. The other day I toted one poor fellow down – he were hale and hearty on Thursday and on Tuesday he were dead.'

So many men, along with women and children, perished from the disease that the church graveyard at Chapel-le-Dale had to be extended.

> 'Twenty pounds are donated towards the cost of enlarging the burial ground at Chapel-le-Dale rendered necessary in consequence of the epidemic smallpox among the navvy population.'
>
> *Midland Railway records*

What happens when you die of smallpox?

DANGEROUS DAYS DEATH VIII

SMALLPOX

Victim: unknown navvy

Smallpox is caused by the Variola major virus and has been around for thousands of years, killing people in very large numbers.

You catch it by close contact with infected people, breathing in the virus on their droplets of spit and snot. Once inside you, the virus multiplies quietly for a week to ten days before you feel a bit fluey with a temperature. Then the spots appear all over, you feel very ill and take to your bed. Over the next few days the spots develop into pustules, oozing fluid over your skin and further ruining your complexion. The virus is overwhelming your internal organs. With your immune system failing, bacteria are taking the once-in-a-lifetime open invitation to feed on your lungs. So having suffered for about ten days, you die. Well, about 30 per cent of people do.

Dr Peter Fox

After the Settle and Carlisle nightmare the railways would start to use steam shovels to replace brute navvy muscle power. Working the railroads would be a little less dangerous. A little.

But the 1870s were to prove the worst decade ever for passenger deaths. Trains were reaching 80 mph now. Stephenson's *Rocket* had been light and slow. But tons of train hitting you at 80 mph would leave you severely dented. One way or another, railways equalled danger.

Did you know … keep the home fire burning

The most popular pub for the Ribblehead navvies was the Gearstones Arms. To liven up an evening session that was proving a little boring, dismal and dull, a navvy decided to throw a stick of dynamite on the fire. You won't be drinking in the Gearstones Arms today.

DERAILING AND DROWNING

⁓ PRICE OF PROGRESS ⁓

> 'Without continual growth and progress, such words as improvement, achievement, and success have no meaning.'
>
> *Benjamin Franklin*

The first trains were about innovation and expansion. Speed was king. The fillings in your teeth may have been shaken out, but you got there quicker than a greyhound on amphetamines. But by the 1880s passenger comfort had become a priority. Those golden days saw dining cars introduced and (on the principle that what goes in must come out) there were toilets in carriages – and corridors to get to them. Some railways got steam radiators to warm the travellers' toes and an improved emergency cord … as well as a bell to summon the guard.

Express trains had always been a first-class luxury, but by 1887 you could travel on express trains in second-class comfort. The peasants could keep pace with the posh.

The 1890s brought in electric lighting on some trains – far safer than the gas that added to the danger in the event of an accident.

Trains had most of the things we take for granted on a rail journey today. The future was looking rosy. Yes there were puny things call automobiles puttering and popping along the roads. The railway companies were confident that they would go the way of the steam-car experiments of 90 years ago. Even a great engineer like Richard Trevithick had failed with a fireball at his only attempt.

Railroads of religion

> 'Houses were knocked down; streets broken through and stopped; deep pits and trenches dug in the ground; enormous heaps of earth and clay thrown up; buildings that were undermined and shaking, propped by great beams of wood. Here, a chaos of carts, overthrown and jumbled together, lay topsy-turvy at the bottom of a steep unnatural hill; there, confused treasures of iron soaked and rusted in something that had accidentally become a pond.'
>
> Dombey and Son, *Charles Dickens*

The coming of the railways flattened streets like Godzilla on the march. They swept away homes and changed lives. But they led to a rash of building too. Places that were once isolated villages became 'suburbs' of the larger towns and cities.

By the 1880s the world was awash with commuters. Instead of living a short walk from their place of employment the workers became accustomed to letting the train take the strain.*

---

* 'Let the train take the strain' was a slogan devised a hundred years later. Commuters of the 1980s played sardines in the morning and evening then went home to see that advert. Oh, how they laughed with childish glee.

A village like Tottenham doubled in size in the 1880s then doubled again the decade later.

But the railways weren't finished with their ravages. Accidents continued to traumatize hundreds.

'Speed Kills. Kill Your Speed,' the 1994 road safety campaign demanded. And speed struck terror into the hearts of many railway watchers ... speed and the fact God had not prophesied the coming of these hissing and hurtling horrors.

> 'Railroads are impossibilities and rank infidelity to the Lord. There is nothing in the Word of God about them. If God had designed that His intelligent creatures should travel at the frightful speed of fifteen miles an hour by steam, He would have clearly foretold it through His holy prophets. It is a device of Satan to lead immortal souls down to hell.'
>
> *American evangelist*

And, lo, God hath not predicted traffic wardens (yet another device to lead immortal souls down to Hell). Mind you, God hath not predicted the *Titanic*, so maybe the old Bible-basher had a point.

Let's hope no one told the preacher man that steam trains went even quicker than the awesome 15 miles an hour. You just *know* that if he saw *Mallard* at 120 mph he'd have cried, 'Duck!' (Oh, please yourself.)

But trains were lethal weapons, as accidents down the years illustrated. The railways needed constant maintenance to eliminate the dangers of faulty machinery. Such as cracked wheels that needed checking ... scientifically.

> WOMAN: 'You may think me a little stupid but why do they tap the wheels?'
>
> WILLIAM PORTER: 'Well, you see, madam, it's like this. If I tap the wheel with this hammer and the wheel goes clang, then I know that the wheel's there.'
>
> MAN: 'But supposing that the wheel doesn't go clang?'
>
> WILLIAM PORTER: 'Well, then I know that the train's gone!'
>
> *From movie* Oh, Mr Porter!

But it was the maintenance that created the most dangerous of days on the railways of Queen Victoria …

— KILLER CRASHES —

Trains went on crashing. Speed has always killed. In 1825 a carriage ran away down a steep hill at Severn Stoke …

> 'Several people were cut, bruised and dreadfully mangled. Two died.'
>
> Manchester Guardian, *report 1825*

But that was a stagecoach crash. When we consider train accidents we have to remember that riding on horseback or in a carriage, or even walking can be fatal.*****

So what were the railway accidents that made the Victorian headlines …

———

* And, according to every school in the universe, running in the corridor is an accident waiting to happen and a fatal accident at that. Many a tragic student has been impaled on a pencil.

The Rednal disaster, 7 June 1865

'Many a trip continues long after movement and space have ceased'

John Steinbeck (1902–68), American novelist

Some one-way tickets are definitely non-return* ... the ones when you reach the end of your lifeline before you reach the end of your train line.

The lyrics of Messrs Lennon and McCartney's song are curious – 'a one-way ticket' (yeah?) – because 'day-trippers' by definition go AND return on the same day. But who are we to argue with the Merseyside poets? Maybe they had some passengers from the Rednal disaster in mind. That was a day-tripper train. An excursion.

Excursions. What an adventure. Sell cheap tickets to trippers and send passengers off to a strange destination town for a great day out. The town traders at the destination can rip off the trapped tourists with tawdry souvenirs and overpriced ices, teas and kiss-me-quick hats. Everyone ends the day happy.

The first 'special' train was probably one run by the Bodmin and Wadebridge Railway in Cornwall in June 1836. The great attraction was a public hanging. Excursions to bare-knuckle fights, where boxers had been known to die, were another grim tripper attraction. The Blackpool illuminations can't compete with such painful pleasures.

The special excursion trains were so popular the railway companies could bring in the bucks by cramming the carriages and then adding more.

On 7 June 1865 the Great Western ran a train to take

---

* Unless you count going home in a pine box as a return, of course.

Victorian Lennons and McCartneys from Birkenhead on Merseyside on an excursion to Shrewsbury. The operators coupled 28 carriages and two brake vans to a pair of locomotives. You could sit at a level crossing and read *War and Peace* while you waited for that lot to shuffle past.

Not enough? The train reached Gobowen and added another four carriages. A lot of people wanted a holiday.

> 'A perpetual holiday is a good working definition of hell.'
>
> *George Bernard Shaw*

This holiday was certainly heading for hell.

Locomotive no. 5 had Driver Anderton at the controls while locomotive no. 72 was driven by Driver Evans.

Meanwhile a gang of labourers was working to make sure the line was in top condition by replacing sections of track at Rednal. The Shrewsbury excursion would be coming over the hill and running towards them around 11.30 that morning, so they placed a green flag on a pole at the top of the hill to let the driver know.

Green for danger.

But 11.30 came and went. The train was late – it would be slow going with all those coaches.

Finally, at 12.29, the excursion reached the top of the hill that overlooked the Rednal track workers 1,000 yards below. The train with Driver Anderton in the lead chugged merrily past the flag and gathered speed, like a jogging rhino, down the slope.

Driver Evans had seen the flag and wondered why Anderton was charging ahead. He gave a toot of his whistle. Driver Anderton seemed as deaf to that as he'd been blind to the flag.

Then Anderton saw the workers. First he blew the shrill whistle to tell them to stand clear. Then he blew the brake whistle to tell his fireman to apply the brakes. He applied the brakes.

Sir Isaac Newton could have explained the laws of physics and something called 'momentum', but Isaac wasn't around.

> 'It should be possible to explain the laws of physics to a barmaid.'
>
> *Albert Einstein (1879–1955), German-born physicist*

It took a lot of energy to get the train up to that speed, and it would take a large and prolonged force to bring it to a stop afterwards. Throw in 'gravity' – that downhill slope – and the lack of friction of iron wheels on iron rails, and you have as much chance of stopping an avalanche in a couple of hundred yards.

Anderton's loco reached the rail works and the front wheels jumped off the track. With 32 coaches pushing it towards its fate, it ground along until it reached Rednal station and hit an obstruction. That slowed it suddenly. The twenty-four rear carriages carried on at speed to crush the first four carriages like a matchbox under a hammer. Eleven other crowded coaches were badly damaged.

Eleven passengers and a fireman died. As Anderton was dug out from the coal that covered him, he said those famous last words:

> 'I didn't see any green flag. There wasn't one.'

He died.

The accident investigator blamed the absurd lack of braking power for such a huge weight of train. And he blamed the inadequate protection offered by a green flag on a pole.

He stipulated there should have been detonators placed

on the line so that, even if a driver missed a visual signal, the loud bangs would give him a warning.

But even detonators could fail when human error entered the laws of physics …

And by cruel coincidence that was demonstrated just two days later in Kent …

The Staplehurst rail crash, 9 June 1865

> 'In the same carriage with me there sat an ancient gentleman who expressed himself most mournfully as to the ruinous effects and rapid spread of railways, and was most pathetic upon the virtues of the slow-going old stage coaches. But I invariably found that when the speed of the train abated, or there was the slightest prolongation of our stay at any station, the old gentleman was up in arms and his watch was instantly out of his pocket, denouncing the slowness of our progress.'
>
> *Charles Dickens*

The Staplehurst disaster was a railway accident in Kent, England. Ten passengers died and forty more were injured. The accident was very similar to the one at Rednal, yet it is far better known. The reason is the Staplehurst crash had celebrity stardust sprinkled over it … and a fair scattering of scandal amid the broken bones and blood and brains.

One of the passengers aboard that day was Charles Dickens, the most famous man in England. Victorians would tell you this man had single-handedly revived the celebration of Christmas with his tale about Mr Scrooge and his ghosts. The ardent readers could tell you about Mr Pickwick's papers and Oliver's gruel life, Copperfield's dark days and the Bleak House of Esther Summerson.

Dickens made hundreds of public appearances as he trailed a few cities, so he was as recognizable as one of today's celebs. He didn't have a gagging order on his private life, but it wasn't widely broadcast. When he was involved in the Staplehurst rail crash one of his greatest fears was that his guilty secret would be broadcast to the Victorian public. His reputation would be as ruined as Wilkins Micawber's and he'd end up like that penurious character in debtors' prison.*

The revelations didn't emerge till years after his death when the corpse of his illicit love was dissected and judged.

> 'A man whose life has been dishonourable is not entitled to escape disgrace in death.'
>
> *Lucius Accius (170–86 BC), Roman poet*

Dickens' mistress, actress Ellen 'Nelly' Ternan, was on the train with him.† She'd been a teenager when they started their affair. Dickens had been 45 and Ms Ternan 18 (the same age as his daughter Katey) when he hired her to take part in a semi-pro theatre show … and he fell for Nell.

If Nell's presence had been broadcast in the newspapers it would have been as shocking as Victoria having a quick smile. You can imagine the headlines … 'Cheating Charlie', 'What the Dickens is he up to?'‡ ''Ell on Wheels'. Or *The Sun*

---

* Or Dickens' own dad. Micawber is based on Dickens' father, John Dickens, who faced similar financial problems when Dickens was a child. The fear of debt haunted the author.

† So was Ellen's mother. They had a chaperone … but there'd still be embarrassing questions for the great man to dodge and duck, sidestep or circumvent. The happiness turned to terror – the best of times became the worst of times (as Dickens almost said).

‡ Not 'Dickens', of course but 'Dickon' – a nickname for the Devil. The phrase had been in use for hundreds of years before Charles was famous.

might go for the more elaborate, 'There's an old train in the stream, Nelly, teen!'

As the happy couple clattered through Kent on their way home from a trip to Paris, disaster struck.

Train wheels screeched against the rails, luggage and passengers were thrown to the floor. The train juddered then, just as it was skidding to a halt, the engine crunched over a low bridge – which collapsed. Most of the following carriages dropped into the stream bed. Charles Dickens was in a carriage at the back that tipped but didn't fall. He was one of the first to recover his wits.

> 'I was in the only carriage that did not go over into the stream. It hung suspended and balanced in an apparently impossible manner. Two ladies were my fellow passengers; an old one, and a young one. The old lady cried out "My God!" and the young one screamed.
>
> 'I caught hold of them both. The young lady said in a frantic way, "Let us join hands and die friends."'
>
> *Charles Dickens, letter to Thomas Mitton, a friend*

Of course the passengers were locked in, according to railway practice at the time. Once the guard freed him, Dickens helped his mistress-muse out of the carriage, along with her mother, then set about rescuing other passengers. It was grim work …

> 'Suddenly I came upon a staggering man covered with blood (I think he must have been flung clean out of his carriage) with such a frightful cut across the skull that I couldn't bear to look at him. I poured some water over his face, and gave him some to

drink, and gave him some brandy, and laid him down on the grass, and he said, "I am gone", and died afterwards.

'Then I stumbled over a lady lying on her back against a little pollard tree, with the blood streaming over her face (which was lead colour) in a number of distinct little streams from the head. I asked her if she could swallow a little brandy, and she just nodded, and I gave her some and left her for somebody else. The next time I passed her, she was dead.

Traumatic.

A man pinned under the carriage was one of the ten to die. Ellen was one of the 40 injured. Dickens laboured for three hours, helping where he could, and was lauded as a hero.

Then the consummate professional climbed back into the perilously and precariously balanced carriage to recover a manuscript of *Our Mutual Friend*. He joked that he had recovered two of the characters, Mr and Mrs Boffin, who had been in the carriage with him. After the crash the writer found them 'much soiled but otherwise unhurt'.

But the impact on the author's psyche was lasting. He concluded his letter to Mitton …

'But in writing these scanty words of recollection, I feel the shake and am obliged to stop.'

For the rest of his life Dickens would try to avoid travel by express trains, and even suffered anxiety when he was travelling by slower, stopping train services. He sometimes got off several stops before his destination and walked the rest of the way.

So how did they end up in a stream and so close to death and disgrace? The old 'human error' again.

☀ The Folkestone Boat Express sailed from France and set off when the tide was high … Since the tide changed every day, so did the Boat Express timetable.

☀ The railway line was being repaired at a spot where it ran across a low bridge over the River Beult. In the belief that the Boat Express train would arrive at 5.20 p.m., foreman John Benge set about taking the rails up. He was mistaken.

☀ Benge set a young lookout, John Wiles, to plant a red flag just in case some unexpected train huffed down the track. But young Wiles was not far enough away to give adequate warning to a fast express train. He was 500 metres down the line instead of 1,000 metres. Mistake 2.

☀ The lookout also had detonators for the line. He should have had three detonators in place 1,000 metres away from the workings. He had two … and was told to use them only if visibility was poor. Mistake 3.

☀ The driver whistled to signal the three brake vans to apply the anchors and threw the train into reverse. Too late. It slid along like jelly on a buttered plate.

☀ The engine managed to reach the far side of the river, running over the beams of the bridge, but the wooden structure cracked, and most of the carriages fell into the shallow waters of the River Beult.

The accident happened on 9 June 1865. Charles Dickens died five years later … on 9 June 1870. Did the shock of the crash shorten the life of Britain's most celebrated author? Certainly he wrote less after the accident. He said, 'I write half a dozen words and turn faint and sick.' Did the dangers of Victoria's railways deprive us of some of the greatest work that was never written? We'll never know.*

The shock to Dickens' system was so great he lost his voice for two weeks. The fear of exposure of his relationship with Nellie was just as great. He strove to make sure no mention of her appeared in the press. 'I don't want to be examined at the Inquests,' he said, the implication being, *I don't want to be asked awkward questions.*

DANGEROUS DAYS DEATH IX

POST TRAUMATIC STRESS

Victim: Charles Dickens

The Staplehurst rail disaster undoubtedly contributed to Dickens' final demise from a stroke.

So how do you die from a stroke? Well, it depends how much of your brain and which bit is affected. You can get away with a small part, but anything that affects the area controlling your heart or breathing for example, that's curtains.

It all starts with a blood clot whizzing along in your blood having a great ride. Not being too big it surfs the bigger blood vessels into your head. Once there it's like bagatelle, carried along on the currents, randomly following a path. All is fine till it enters a blood vessel that is slightly smaller than itself. Then it's stuck, blocking the

---

* He wrote no more of the great novels. Only half of the unfinished *Mystery of Edwin Drood*. A whodunnit. Whodunnit? Something else we'll never know.

> supply of blood, oxygen and nutrients to that area of the brain. Brain cells are very sensitive souls; without oxygen and food they die and the messages they send gradually stop. And if there are no messages to your heart … it's goodnight Vienna.
>
> Dr Peter Fox

And the simple human errors that caused such chaos?

The foreman, John Benge, DID check the Boat Express timetable – but he was looking at the page for the day before.

His head carpenter also had a timetable showing when the express was due. He had dropped it on a rail and an earlier train had destroyed it.

Doh. And double doh.

Did you know … dangerous driving director

In the 1840s a director of the London and Greenwich Railway missed his train. He commandeered a locomotive from the station and set off in pursuit of his train. He was so successful he not only caught it but ran into the back of it. The force was so great it broke the legs of a couple of passengers.

More haste, zero speed.

The Newmarket Arch crash, 6 June 1851 and 6 June 1852

Mr Dickens was not the only victim of the anniversary curse.

On 6 June 1852, a train was running between Brighton and Lewes when it struck a sleeper that had been laid across the track. A gang of workers were in the area, leaving sleepers alongside the track, but the nearest worker was a few hundred yards away. The train derailed and fell onto the road, killing two crew and three passengers.

Sabotage! And the chief suspect was little Jimmy Boakes who lived in a cottage alongside the track. The police superintendent grilled little Jimmy relentlessly but the boy denied it … and, anyway, how could a ten-year-old lift a three-metre sleeper?

An unsolved mystery.

On 6 June 1852, one year later to the day, little Jimmy went again to view the scene of the accident. He was struck by a bolt of lightning and killed. The Big Sleep for little Jimmy of the big sleeper maybe? Justice?

> 'To me belongeth vengeance, and recompense; their foot shall slide in due time: for the day of their calamity is at hand, and the things that shall come upon them make haste.'*****
>
> *Deuteronomy 32:35*

The Menheniot crash, Cornwall 1873

He was a cheerful chap, the signalman at Menheniot, and knew most of the train crew by name. Most. Two trains were waiting to depart – one on the 'up' line and one on the 'down' line.

---

* That is reassuring, then. We can leave it to God to zap the unrighteous. He probably turned Jack the Ripper into Jack the crisp, which is why the Whitechapel weirdo was never caught. But in little Jimmy's case, God, why didn't you frazzle him BEFORE he killed five people? Just wondering. Yes, I know, you move in wondrous ways …

It was a single track so he had to be careful. It wouldn't do to send that 'up' train off when another train was heading 'down' – they would meet head on. But it was safe enough to send the 'down' train away.

There was no signal to command the trains. Everything relied on telegraph messages to the signalman, who passed them on verbally.

The cheerful signalman chap received the all-clear on the 'down' line and called to the guard on the waiting 'down' train, 'Off you go, Dick.'

How was the signalman to know that the 'up' train guard was also called Dick? Oh, the horror the cheerful one must have felt as he watched that 'up' train steam off towards a head-on crash with an oncoming 'down' train.

In the inevitable collision a driver died.

> 'God created profoundly fallible creatures on this earth, and human history is mostly the story of error and accident.'
>
> *Michael Ledeen (1941—), American historian*

Thorpe Station crash, 1874

'All right.' Two little words. Twenty-five deaths.

On a rainy night in Norfolk the mail train from London was late. The mail train was waiting to set off along the single line in the opposite direction.

The inspector in the telegraph office suggested they let the mail train come into the station.

The stationmaster refused. But the inspector decided to give him an argument. 'We can hold the express train another 20 minutes.'

The stationmaster snapped, 'All right.' Meaning, 'All right, I've heard enough of your lip, just do as I told you.'

The inspector thought he meant, 'All right, I agree with you.' He sent a telegraph message and the mail train was sent on its way.

The express pulled into the station. A different inspector gave it permission to leave … into the path of the mail train. 'You TOLD me to!' the inspector wailed when they realized what had happened.

We don't know what happened in the last moments before the two trains met. The crews died. But in the wreckage the regulators were found to be screwed shut on the locomotives. In the final few moments the drivers must have seen their terrifying fate, looming through the fine rain.

Their last words were certainly not, 'All right.'

> 'Mistakes are a part of being human. Precious life lessons that can only be learned the hard way. Unless it's a fatal mistake, which, at least, others can learn from.'
>
> *Al Franken (1951—), American comedian*

The Foxcote crash, 1876

> 'He cuts a corner so closely now and then that I feel myself "scrooching", as the children say.'
>
> *Mark Twain*, Innocents Abroad, *1869*

We call it 'cutting corners' – 'To do something in the easiest or most inexpensive way, often discarding normal safe practice in order to get fast results.'

It's not unusual. But when the Victorian railways did it the results could prove fatal ... though not to the people with the money. A good way to economize is to hire cheap labour. Hire young people who work long hours for low pay. The down side is they have little experience or training because training costs money. Put three young lads together and you have a recipe for pain and suffering. The three concerned were ...

- Herbert John – age 18 – working 6.30 a.m. to 9.30 p.m. for 17 shillings and 6 pence a week – in charge of signals at Radstock.

- Alfred Dando – almost illiterate and unable to read telegraph messages – in his post four months – so weak he couldn't pull the signal-box levers to signal danger – left in charge of Foxcote signal-box with insufficient paraffin to light the signal lamps.*

- Arthur Hillard – age 15 – working 8 a.m. to 10 p.m. in theory but usually longer – wage 7 shillings and 6 pence per week – in charge of the telegraph at Wellow (when not collecting tickets or doing station accounts).

Trains between Radstock and Wellow (passing through Foxcote) were at the tender mercies of these three boys.

It was 7 August and the height of the holiday season so there were 17 extra trains (mostly excursions packed with fun-seekers) for the lads to cope with. It was 15-year-old Arthur Hillard who allowed one train to enter his section then another from the opposite direction ... head-on crash. The sound was heard five miles away and the whistling of

---

* When he knew a train was coming he simply walked out of the signal-box, waved a hand-held lantern and told the driver it was safe to carry on.

the engines haunted the midnight air till all their steam was gone. It was a keening, macabre threnody to the 12 trippers who died.

Young Arthur wasn't left to shoulder all the blame. The inspector, Captain Tyler, blamed the railway company …

'Railway working under such conditions cannot be expected to result in anything *other* than serious accidents.'

New electrical devices were invented to make sure collisions on single-line railways could never happen again.

'Wise men profit more from fools than fools from wise men.'

Cato the Elder (234–149 BC), Roman statesman

The Wigan disaster, 1873

Queen Victoria loved rail travel but was a nervous passenger. She decreed that no matter how fast engines could run *her* train would not exceed 40 mph.

'To suffer the penalty of too much haste, which is too little speed.'

Plato (427–347 BC), Greek philosopher

'What good is speed if the brain has oozed out on the way?'

St Jerome (AD 347–420), Christian historian

An accident occurred at Wigan that allowed her to say, 'I told you so.'

The train involved was the one carrying HM's holiday necessities and her entourage up to Balmoral for her summer holiday. It would travel up the west coast route while Victoria usually travelled up the east coast line. The two lines saw themselves in competition … and competition breeds carelessness.

Part of the entourage's train derailed at Wigan station. The cause remains a mystery but excessive speed is one of the chief suspects. Why was the driver in a hurry? To prove his company was faster and more efficient, perhaps? What happened?

> The driver saw sparks from the tail of his 25-coach train as they passed through Wigan in the early hours of 2 August 1873. He stopped gently and walked back to investigate.

> The middle coaches of the train had jumped off the track and run along the platform of Wigan station, scattering luggage and wrecking the canopy.

> The rear part of the train had come loose and some of the coaches lay upside down, wheels in the air like dead sheep. Several passengers were dead.

> One carriage had smashed through the wall at the side of the track and fallen onto the roof of an iron foundry below.

> A servant in the carriage, Mrs Roberts, was thrown through the roof of the foundry and her fall was broken by the concrete floor.

The wrecked carriages were detached and left for rescuers

to remove the 13 dead and help the 30 injured. The sleeping people in the front part of the train were taken on to Scotland. They were only told about the tragedy when they awoke the next morning.*****

The inquiry blamed the points at the station even though investigators could find nothing wrong with them. Survivors blamed speed and said they'd felt the train was going recklessly and rashly quick. What were those drivers? Boiler aces or boy racers?**†**

Did you know ... Vic's tantrum

The High Level Bridge over the River Tyne was opened in 1849 by Queen Victoria. (Along with Robert Stephenson's Tweed Bridge, opened the next year, it would complete the line from London to Edinburgh.)

A banquet was held in the Station Hotel in Newcastle to celebrate. After the feast it is said the hotel manager presented Queen Vic with the bill for the dinner. Thereafter the furious queen refused to look upon the disgraced city and drew her carriage curtains closed every time she passed through.

---

* I don't know about you, but I think I'd like to know that my colleagues in the back section of my train had been killed and maimed. Then the driver could ask me if I'd like to carry on travelling in a train that had just had a fatal accident.

† In the 21st century the East Coast and West Coast routes were still vying to be the fastest. Virgin Trains, on the West Coast, introduced 'Pendolino' carriages that tilted on bends ... and made some passengers seasick. A Pendolino crash at Grayrigg in 2007 killed one person. A points failure was blamed. Sound familiar?

Train power

In a contest between train and human, the train usually wins.

In 1833 a locomotive on the Liverpool and Manchester line broke down in a cloud of steam. Passengers stepped out of their carriages to see what the problem might be. Through the clouds of steam they failed to see the train on the parallel track approaching.

> 'They accordingly came upon them with fearful violence; several were knocked down and the wheels of the train passed over four of them. Three of the unfortunate party were killed on the spot, their bodies being dreadfully crushed. Recovery of the fourth is considered hopeless.'
>
> The Times, *February 1833*

In 1884 a guard on a Midland Railway train from Liverpool reported he'd heard a loud knocking under his van as it passed through the Haddon tunnel at 50 mph. When the train stopped at Derby, the driver examined the locomotive, finding 'blood and brains' on the front of the engine and a scrap of cloth wrapped around a pipe.

A search of the tunnel revealed the dismembered remains of a 'working man' scattered over a distance of several hundred metres. You have to wonder what the 'working man' was doing in the tunnel at 11 p.m.

Careless walk costs lives.

‑ WATERY GRAVES ‑

'When you're drowning, you don't say "I would be incredibly pleased if someone would have the foresight to notice me drowning and come and help me," you just scream.'

John Lennon

Trains don't run through rivers. They go over them or under them. The tunnels killed the navvies but the bridges killed the passengers when they collapsed … when the bridges collapsed, not the passengers, that is.

The catalogue of bridge disasters is a sorry story.

1   The River Medway disaster

It was a stormy night … it often was in bridge disaster stories or Hammer Horror movies. The River Medway was in full spate. It was spating so fully it washed away part of the Medway Bridge on the line between Tunbridge and Penshurst. A South East Railways goods train plunged into the river. The injured driver was dragged out by the brave fireman, but died soon after.

'It takes just one big natural disaster to remind us that, here on Earth, we're still at the mercy of nature.'

Neil deGrasse Tyson, American astrophysicist (1958—)

As usual we don't know the name of the driver because he was of the labouring classes. But Anon Driver was almost certainly the first victim of the first rail bridge disaster.

2   The Dee Bridge disaster

Disasters can bring unlikely heroes into the spotlight. In 1846 there was a bridge failure on Robert Stephenson's railway at Chester. An engine driver felt the line tremble beneath him and suspected the bridge was about to collapse. He accelerated and drove the locomotive to safety as a girder toppled into the River Dee below. The tender was torn away, along with the rest of the train. Four died and sixteen were injured in the plunge.*

The driver drove on to the next station to summon help. But he realized that following trains would take a dive when they reached the broken girder. So he headed back on the parallel line, over the bridge that had just killed his colleagues, and saved untold lives. That took nerve.

> 'Courage is being scared to death ... and saddling up anyway.'
>
> *John Wayne (1907–79), American film actor*

Sometimes a man's gotta do what a man's gotta do.†

---

* The use of cast iron for bridges was suddenly in doubt. Robert Stephenson was shaken by the inquiry's report ... though not as shaken as the passengers.

† As John Wayne didn't say. He DID say, 'Well, there's some things a man just can't run away from.' Actor Charlton Heston claimed he said the famous line in the movie *Three Violent People* ... but the truth is he said, 'A man must do what he must do' ... which doesn't have the same ring to it.

3   The Cornwall Railway bridge disaster

The travelling public looked on the wooden trestles and trembled.* There were 34 of them on the Cornwall Railway between Plymouth and Truro. 'They'll collapse, just like the Medway,' the prophets of doom predicted when the line opened in 1859. They were wrong … but just two days after the line opened a locomotive was derailed and toppled over into the muddy stream, ten metres below. It lay there, on its back, like a tranquillized deer. The name of the locomotive was *Elk*. This time the fireman was too dead to rescue the driver and the driver too dead to return the favour. The guard died as well, but 14 passengers survived to tell the tale … and probably put the fear of steam into their neighbours.

> 'Character is much easier kept than recovered.'
>
> *Thomas Paine (1737–1809), English-American author and revolutionary*

4   The Tay Bridge disaster

The biggie. The one everyone remembers … though the details are forgotten. Of course it owed some of its fame to the magnificently putrid poet McGonagall.†

---

* There were a lot of valleys to be bridged in Cornwall, and wood was cheaper than iron. But the maintenance proved high. The iconic wooden bridges were eventually replaced.

† William Topaz wrote such spectacularly bad poetry there have been attempts to explain his style. Some say he suffered Asperger's Syndrome. But most interesting is the theory he was a highly intelligent writer who made his name with a deliberate hoax – he KNEW exactly how deadly his doggerel was. He died penniless … but so did Van Gogh. Like Van Gogh he is remembered in the popular public minds long after the allegedly talented contemporaries are all but forgotten.

> 'Beautiful Railway Bridge of the Silv'ry Tay!
> Alas! I am very sorry to say
> That ninety lives have been taken away
> On the last Sabbath day of 1879,
> Which will be remember'd for a very long time.'
>
> *William Topaz McGonagall (1825–1902)*

How could it all go so wrong?

➤ The bridge over the Tay was designed by Thomas Bouch with brick piers on a rock base. The bed of the river proved more unstable than he thought – more gravel than rock – so he switched to cast iron. (The ghost of Robert Stephenson should have warned Bouch of the weakness of cast iron after the Dee disaster.) But look on the bright side, it was *cheaper*.

➤ The alignment of the girders and braces was 'adjusted' when they didn't quite meet. Rather than the word 'adjusted' you may prefer the word 'bodged'. A witness at the subsequent inquiry said, 'It was about as slovenly a piece of work as ever I saw in my life.' Bad planning AND bad construction then.

➤ A Board of Trade inspector was appointed, one Major-General Hutchinson. He watched six locomotives run over the bridge and declared it safe. 'I wish I had the opportunity of seeing a train cross it in a high wind,' he lamented. But he couldn't whistle up a wind so he guesstimated it would be all right. This optimistic bridge inspector was later questioned. How could he have certified it as fit? It turned out that the Major-General had no qualifications and no experience. He wouldn't have spotted a faulty bridge if it had fallen on his head.

➢ The bridge opened in June 1878 and Queen Victoria herself graced it with a trip across. She was given a gun salute, which must have sounded ominously like cracking girders. If it didn't collapse under the queen's bulk, surely it never would. But Victoria didn't have wind … for her crossing.

➢ Engineer Thomas Bouch was given a knighthood and everything was hunky-dory. Until 18 months had passed and the bridge was tested by that rigorous inspector of human endeavours, Mother Nature.

Maintenance was placed in the hands of Henry Noble. Mr Noble was, fatally, not an engineer. He was a bricklayer. When workmen noticed the bridge vibrate they whacked in a few wedges and hoped they'd hold. They did. For 18 months.

On the evening of 29 December 1879 a gale erupted. The worst the region had seen for 30 years with speeds of maybe 80 mph. It swept across Scotland and caused enormous damage. It reached the Tay valley and found the frail bridge of Bouch in its path. The hurricane was at right angles to the shoddy girders.

'There is really no such thing as bad weather, only different kinds of good weather.'

John Ruskin (1819–1900), English writer and painter

Mr Ruskin was not standing on the Tay Bridge on 29 December 1879.

The train that evening was pulled by a new and superior locomotive, no. 224, as the regular little engine had broken down. The signalman at South Fort station, at the south end of the bridge, handed the driver a token that allowed him to pass along the single line. The wind was so fierce the man had to crawl back to his signal box on all fours.

He watched the train lights shrink into the night. A sudden gust clattered his cabin, he saw a flash of light from the bridge followed by Bible blackness. He tried to walk to the bridge but was blown back. He went down to the sheltered shore of the Tay and at that moment the moon broke through the clouds. It showed a mangled and tangled wreckage of girders. There was no train.

Seventy-five people, including the train crew, went to feed the fishes. Only forty-six bodies were ever recovered.

The ghouls gathered, as they did at most disasters before and since. The morning after the storm 'many thousand persons congregated around the station buildings and strong men and women are wringing their hands in despair,' *The Times* reported.

Some unsympathetic English prophets of doom said it served the passengers right for being wicked enough to travel on a Sunday. In a racial reverse, the Scottish foundry that cast the girders complained they had to use inferior iron from Middlesbrough, England. They'd have preferred 'good Scotch metal'.

A court of inquiry turned just as much savagery on Thomas Bouch.

> 'We find that the bridge was badly designed, badly constructed and badly maintained. For these defects Sir Thomas Bouch is in our opinion mainly to blame.'

Ouch, Bouch. Sir Thomas died just ten months after the bridge collapsed, a broken man with his reputation as an engineer ruined. The design was indeed his responsibility – but perhaps the builders and maintenance team could have

DANGEROUS DAYS DEATH X

DROWNING

Victim: David Mitchell,
driver of the train that plunged into the Tay ✱

You hit the water hard, the force of which punches the air out of your lungs as you submerge into the darkness below. Immediately you start to gasp uncontrollably as the ancient, inbuilt 'diving' reflex takes over. Blood is moved to your heart and head from the rest of your body. Your breathing becomes fast and uncontrolled, leading to gulping water into your lungs. Your brain begins to feel as if it's on fire. Oxygen starved, the brain cells die. Quickly you become unconscious and peace reigns as you finally sink slowly into the depths to die.

Around 1 in 5 people die this way in very cold water, usually within minutes, so it's reasonably quick and relatively painless as deaths go. Of course you may be unlucky and be in the other group who survive longer, providing of course you can reach the surface and breathe.

If that's you, then you are in for around 15–30 minutes of mind-numbing cold. Slowly you lose body heat. Again to protect your precious brain, blood is diverted from your extremities to your heart and the central major blood supply routes to the head. With little blood left in the arms and legs they become useless to you. Unable to swim and being so cold, you lose consciousness. Exhausted, like a rag doll, you finally slip beneath the water and drown.

Dr Peter Fox

✱ He ended up in an unmarked grave in his home town of Leslie. In 2011 a campaign raised the money to commemorate his death with a new headstone. One less 'forgotten hero' of the railway age.

shared the liability and the guilt? His design for the Forth Rail Bridge was not used. The Forth fishes stayed hungry.

Bouch was probably spared the gloating of the poet McGonagall who (with the wisdom of hindsight) managed a pompously preaching tone when he whinnied …

> 'Your central girders would not have given way,
> At least many sensible men do say,
> Had they been supported on each side with buttresses,
> At least many sensible men confesses,
> For the stronger we our houses do build,
> The less chance we have of being killed.'

Locomotive no. 224 was hauled out – despite being carelessly dropped back in – twice. It was finally recovered and repaired. The sick Scottish railwaymen nicknamed it *The Diver*, though many superstitious drivers were loath to take it over the new bridge. It carried on working for another 40 years.

The masonry piers that held the ill-fated bridge can still be seen. A reminder of something which will be remember'd for a very long time.

5   The Forth Bridge triumph

After the horror of the Tay Bridge Disaster the Forth Bridge was designed and built with more care. But the human cost of the build was still high. It was begun in 1883.

The jolly jesting chaps who built the bridge very often brought about their own demise. They would warm themselves with strong drink, which deceived them into thinking they could jump the gaps between the girders.

'First you take a drink, then the drink takes a drink, then the drink takes you.'*

F. Scott Fitzgerald

When they failed, the river was there to break their fall … or break their bodies. There were so many falls the contractors deployed a boat to gather in the fallers, or their corpses. Forty died in falls but the workforce was 4,600 so it was a low mortality rate compared to many.

Sinking the support columns required primitive compression chambers that accounted for another 17 deaths.

The Prince of Wales opened the bridge in 1890. Fifty-seven men may have died in the building but 300 skylarks died to make the pie that the tubby prince guzzled at the celebration banquet.†

'Hark! Hark! The lark at heaven's gate sings.'

William Shakespeare

The poor tweeter was probably singing at Heaven's gate because it was too dead to sing on Earth. The new bridge, along with the rebuilt Tay Bridge, led to a new speed-war between rival railway companies in 1895.‡ It allowed the

---

* Or, if you're a bridge-builder, you end up in the drink.
† The corpulent Prince of Wales survived an assassination attempt from a Belgian anarchist, protesting about the Boer War. The 15-year-old assassin shot at the prince and missed. He fired twice through the window of a railway carriage as it stood at Brussels station. Not only did he miss the huge sitting target of Prince Edward, he missed everyone else in the compartment. That teenage tearaway was in serious need of target practice.
‡ The speeds were achieved by cutting times at stations as well as rushing along the rails. A porter at Crewe was helping an old lady stack her luggage when the train pulled away. He ended up, an unwilling passenger, in Glasgow. Oh, Mr Porter …

grouse hunters to race up to Scotland and get their kill back to England in record time.

The 1890s were not a good year to be incarnated as a bird.

There had been a warning of sorts. On 2 October 1877, while the bridge was still under construction, one of the girders was blown down during a gale similar to that of 28 December, but 'only' one of the workmen lost his life.

BRIEF TIMELINE – THE NINETIES

1890   The underground goes electric.

1892   Easter Monday crowds descend upon Hampstead Heath railway station … and trample two women and six children to death.

1893   Traffic congestion in Liverpool sorted by an overhead railway system at the riverside. Scousers call it the Dockers' Umbrella.

1894   Helium gas is discovered, but no one is laughing when death duties are imposed to tax your inheritance. Old Vic objects but the laws will be passed. The cost of dying just went up.

1895   Oscar Wilde jailed for his relationship with Lord Alfred Douglas and goes to Reading Gaol.

1896   Britain's first moving picture show is projected at the Olympia Theatre. Glasgow has its own underground system the noo. The railway up Snowdon in Wales is hailed as a miracle … till two trains run out of control and collide, leaving 100 injured. Speed limit raised to 20 mph for cars.*

---

* And, tragically, this meant unemployment for the men with red flags who had walked in front of cars. Like the cars, a 20 mph flag man would be exhausted.

1897   Bram Stoker's *Dracula* is published but there are no vampires to stop Queen Vic, who now celebrates 60 years on the throne. The first man arrested for drunken driving is a taxi driver ... surely not. The first motor fatality is a fortnight later. A nine-year-old boy is run down. By a taxi driver. Would you believe it?

1899   Marylebone station opens as the London terminus of the Great Central Railway. The last major route and the great days of train expansion are long past. Percy Pilcher, pioneer of glider flight, crashes in Leicestershire and dies.

1901   Queen Victoria dies. The end of an era ... literally.

EPILOGUE

'We will be known forever by the tracks we leave.'

Native American proverb

'The Queen must again bring most seriously and earnestly before Mr Gladstone and the Cabinet the very alarming and serious state of the railways. Every day almost everybody trembles for their friends and for every one's life.'

Queen Victoria, letter to Gladstone, 3 October 1873

Victoria died in 1901 but in her lifetime she had seen the most revolutionary face of the Industrial Revolution. The railways.

Cheap, fast travel for even the poorest Brits.* The railways made day-trippers and commuters. Their world would never be the same.

---

* Unless you count the cost in buckets of navvy blood, of course. In which case it was a rather expensive form of transport.

> 'The traveller sees what he sees. The tourist sees what
> he has come to see.'
>
> *G. K. Chesterton (1874–1936), British writer, critic*

In 1848 many of Britain's European neighbours had been trembling under the terrors of political revolutions. Britain just trembled under the hammers and shovels of the railway navigators, the collapsing tunnels, the thundering trains … and the odd exploding one.

The British workers turned their energies to dynamiting the green and pleasant land instead of dynamiting the aristocrats. There *were* lots of forgotten riots on neglected corners of dis-remembered streets. But the big revolution was the industrial one. It was led by the forgotten underclasses of the neglected families of the disremembered workers.*

> 'Almost all the noblest things that have been achieved
> in the world, have been achieved by poor men; poor
> scholars, poor professional men, poor artisans and
> artists, poor philosophers, poets, and men of genius.'
>
> *Albert Pike (1809–91), American attorney*

The train travellers and the tourists of Victoria's Britain forgot the sufferings and enjoyed the journeys. We still do. We take the builders, the inventors and the gambling inves-tors for granted, and grumble when the trains are late. The lateness isn't remarkable – it is the fact the railways exist at all that is a wonder.†

---

* Railways had first-, second- and third-class carriages and the word 'class' – working-, upper- or middle-class – came to be used to describe social status as a result.

† Remember that and let it comfort you. Of course this fine sentiment is no consolation whatsoever to ME when I am standing cold, weary and abandoned by God and railway staff on a King's Cross platform on a wintery night.

The trains – the locomotives and the lines – are better remembered than the men and women who worked, and died, to make them happen.***** The romance of the railways inspired poets to flights of fancy as their rhythms clattered along …

> 'Faster than fairies, faster than witches,
> Bridges and houses, hedges and ditches …
> Here is a cart runaway in the road
> Lumping along with man and load …
> And here is a mill, and there is a river:
> Each a glimpse and gone forever!' **†**
>
> 'From a Railway Carriage',
> Robert Louis Stevenson (1850–94), Scottish novelist and poet

Lumping poetry.**‡** (When will someone write a poem about railways that *doesn't* have a tumpity-tum rhythm?) And where are the poems for the heroes of the revolution? **§**

There are the works of the Navvy Poet. There is even an awful schoolboy effort that was entered for a competition …

---

* 94.78 per cent of the population have heard of the *Flying Scotsman* and *Rocket*, but only 3.2 per cent of Richard Trevithick and 0.00001 per cent of John Cree. (Statistics from the DOG – Department of Guesstimations.)
† They are clearly NOT 'gone forever'. They'll still be there when the next train passes, Robert Louis – no relation to Robert Stephenson. Maybe there should be a campaign to ban this misleading poem from children's anthologies. Poetic licence? Bah, humbug.
‡ The Trades Union of Fairies and Witches responded by pointing out that, while they may be slower than a train, they never break down and have a better record of punctuality. (The tooth fairy always gets through.)
§ All right, it's tough to rhyme with Trevithick … but Watt is not, yet he's forgot by poetic lot, not a jot, memory left to rot, eh what, Watt?

> 'There are on it employed, which cannot be denied
> Some men with great muscular power;
> They work very hard, some work by the yard,
> And others are paid by the hour.'
>
> *Charles Gledhill, schoolboy poet, on navvies*
> *on the Huddersfield and Manchester Railway (1849)*

Of course Victoria exited the drama, stage right, but the railways would go on having their highs and lows. The high being 1913 when the network reached its maximum 20,000 miles, and the low being when Dr Beeching (1913–85) took a hatchet and chopped it by 6,000 miles. But somebody had to do it.

The unregulated tangle of tracks had become a financial liability by the 1960s. Yet people clung to the romance of rail travel and booed and hissed at Doctor Beeching. Like the Black Rat in the plague years, it's time someone rescued Dr Beeching's reputation. Lines were closing long before he became chairman of British Railways – over 3,000 miles had gone before Beeching took up the axe.

This time the popular poets had a go at the sadness of closing stations …

> 'The grass grows high
> At Dog Dyke, Tumby Woodside
> And Trouble House Halt.' *****
>
> *'Slow Train', Flanders and Swann, British comedy duo (1963)*

---

* Trouble House Halt only opened in 1959 and closed in 1964. A short life but a merry one. Trouble was NOT its middle name. 'Trouble House' was a pub. Yes, a pub had its own platform. Drink-drive campaigners must have applauded.

The 'effort and sacrifices' required to build that railway system were enormous. It liberated people around the world and the price was measured in lives.

'Give me blood, and I shall give you freedom.'

Subhas Chandra Bose (1897–1945), Indian nationalist leader

As years passed the railway builders in Victoria's Britain learned from their mistakes, so Britain has one of the safest transport systems in the world. Sadly, the railway operators have struggled to learn from *their* mistakes.

That 1825 first passenger train suffered a mechanical fault. It was an hour late. An hour. Shocking. Surely that can't happen on today's modern railways? No it can't. That miserable hour has extended to over four hours for some unlucky passengers – they'd be dancing on the platform if they were just an hour late.

'Passengers packed into sweltering carriages, overflowing toilets, clueless staff and police called to quell a mutiny: My Bank Holiday nightmare on Britain's Third World railways. Nearly eight hours later, on a trip that should have taken three hours 40 minutes, they had still not reached their final destination. Those going on to Edinburgh eventually arrived at 3.39 a.m., which means passengers who were on the 6 p.m. from London had been travelling for nearly ten hours.'

Mark Palmer, Daily Mail, *26 May 2013*

Which may go to prove…

'We learn from history that we do not learn from history.'

Georg Wilhelm Friedrich Hegel (1770–1831), German philosopher

The author and publisher are grateful to Shutterstock for permission to reproduce images on each chapter opening (©Andrey Kuzmin), and on pages 3 (©Ivor Golovniov), 28 (©Morphart Creation), 215 (©A. Kaiser), 226 (©Hein Nouwens) and 259 (©Oleg Golovnev).

INDEX

Coming Soon
The third instalment in
the Dangerous Days series

The Elizabethan Age was a Golden Age in history, wasn't it?
Glitzy gold, wicked weed and priceless potatoes…

Not really. These were dangerous days. If you survived
the villains, and the diseases didn't get you, then the forces
of law might. Pick the wrong religion, and the stake
or the scaffold awaited you…

Once again, what we think we know about our history
is revealed to be a mish-mash of misconceptions, glory-hogging
and downright untruths as Terry Deary explodes the myths that
permeate our understanding of the past – with a healthy dash
of pitch-black humour.

Find out more at www.orionbooks.co.uk